She.

Other titles from Blanc Press:
Dubious, I by Robert Darry
My Beautiful Beds by Stephanie Rioux
A House on a Hill (A House on a Hill, Part One) by Harold Abramowitz
*All Bodies Are The Same and
    They Have The Same Reactions* by Allison Carter
But On Geometric by Joseph Mosconi
Loquela by Allyssa Wolf
Viva Miscegenation by Brian Kim Stefans
On the Substance of Disorder by Will Alexander
I Fell in Love With a Monster Truck by Amanda Ackerman
Politicized Pretty Picture by Stan Apps
I Can Feel by Teresa Carmody
Forcible Oral Copulation by Vanessa Place
Fried Chicken Dinner by Janice Lee
Tramps Everywhere by Amina Cain
Fur Birds by Michelle Detorie
Kept Women by Kate Durbin
Pieces of Water by Michael Smoler
Airline Music by Amarnath Ravva
My Little Neoliberal Pony by K. Lorraine Graham
Break Bloom Burn by Maximus Kim
The Missing Link by Jen Hofer
Pre-Symbolic by Brian Ang
Erotic in Czech Republic by Ara Shirinyan
Complex Textual Legitimacy Proclamation by Mathew Timmons

She.

by Mathew Timmons

Blanc
Press

Los Angeles

She.
Blanc Press, December 2006

This text was assembled from books written by dead white men, obvious books from the canon that the author of this collection has never read before. These texts are now in the public domain and are readily available from Project Gutenberg: *A Tale of Two Cities* by Charles Dickens, *The Complete Diary of Samuel Pepys* by Samuel Pepys, *The King James Bible*, *Moby Dick* by Herman Melville, *Sister Carrie* by Theodore Dreiser, and *Ulysses* by James Joyce.

She.

She ...

She abandoned the thought of appealing to the other department stores andnow wandered on, feeling a certain safety and relief in mingling with the crowd.

She acknowledged that she had not.

She acknowledged their homage by bending her head, and giving them a quick look.

She acquiesced, and he went.

She acquiesced, however, and he took her name and address.

She actually started.

She admired: a natural phenomenon having been explained by him to her she expressed the immediate desire to possess without gradual acquisition a fraction of his science, the moiety, the quarter, a thousandth part.

She almost forgot poor Drouet, who babbled on as if he were the host.

She almost loved Lola for the sympathy and praise she extended.

She almost trembled at the audacity which might have carried her on to a terrible rebuff.

She also bestowed a British cough on Madame Defarge; but, neither of the two took much heed of her.

She also carried a shining shield.

She also entertained me with repeating many of her own and others' parts of the play-house, which she do most excellently; and tells me the whole practices of the play-house and players, and is in every respect most excellent company.

She also imagined that he took it on her account.

She also is to look out again for another little girle, the last we had being also gone home the very same day she came.

She also lieth in wait as for a prey, and increaseth the transgressors among men.

She also marvelled at the whistles of the hundreds of vessels in the harbour--the long, low cries of the Sound steamers and ferry-boats when fog was on.

- She also noticed that he was smooth-shaven, good looking, and young, but nothing more.

- She also saw that she was not well dressed--not nearly as well dressed--as Mrs. Vance.

- She also took me to her lodging at an Ironmonger's in King Street, which was but very poor, and I found by a letter that she shewed me of her husband's to the King, that he is a right Frenchman, and full of their own projects, he having a design to reform the universities, and to institute schools for the learning of all languages, to speak them naturally and not by rule, which I know will come to nothing.

She also washed my feet in a bath of herbs, and so to bed.

She also washed my feet in a bath of herbs, and so to bed.

She also washed my feet in a bath of herbs, and so to bed.

SHE ALWAYS KEPT THINGS DECENT IN THE HANNIGAN FAMILEYE.

- She always made a bargain for it, by holding up, as a statement of its just price, one finger less than the merchant held up, whatever his number might be.

- She and her father would unquestionably be guilty of this crime, and this woman (the inveteracy of whose pursuit cannot be described) would wait to add that strength to her case, and make herself doubly sure.

- She and I did cast about how to get Captain Grove for my sister, in which we are mighty earnest at present, and I think it would be a good match, and will endeavour it.

She and I singing, and, God forgive me! I do still see that my nature is not to be quite conquered, but will esteem pleasure above all things, though yet in the middle of it, it has reluctances after my business, which is neglected by my following my pleasure.

She and I walked to my Lady's at the Wardrobe, and there dined and was exceeding much made of.

She and Jerry had beheld the coach start, had known who it was that Solomon brought, had passed some ten minutes in tortures of suspense, and were now concluding their arrangements to follow the coach, even as Madame Defarge, taking her way through the streets, now drew nearer and nearer to the else-deserted lodging in which they held their consultation.

She and no other.

She answered.

She answered before them all, that he did not stay so late abroad with her, for he went betimes thence (though he do not before one, two, or three in the morning), but must stay somewhere else.

She answered: --Miss Kennedy, was Mr Boylan in while I was upstairs? She asked.

She answered, slighting: --Ask no questions and you'll hear no lies. Like lady, ladylike.

She answered that she could readily obey what her father and mother had done; which was all she could say, or I expect.

She answered that she had not.

She answered, we were not so well acquainted yet.

(SHE ARCHES HER BODY IN LASCIVIOUS CRISPATION, PLACING HER FOREFINGER IN HER MOUTH)

She arose and tried to push out into the aisle--anywhere.

She arranged a few things hastily and then left for the theatre, half expecting to encounter him at the door.

She arrayed herself most carefully and they started off, extending excuses upstairs.

She asked him was that so.

She asked me where she was, and I told her; who I was, and I told her.

She asked Minnie for ink and paper, which were upon the mantel in the dining-room, and when the latter had gone to bed at ten, got out Drouet's card and wrote him.

She asked you who was in your room.

"She asks only in return," said Carrie, scarcely hearing the small, scheduled reply of her lover, and putting herself even more in harmony with the plaintive melody now issuing from the orchestra, "that when you look upon her your eyes shall speak devotion; that when you address her your voice shall be gentle, loving, and kind; that you shall not despise her because she cannot understand all at once your vigorous thoughts and ambitious designs; for, when misfortune and evil have defeated your greatest purposes, her love remains to console you. You look to the trees," she continued, while Hurstwood restrained his feelings only by the grimmest repression, "for strength and grandeur; do not despise the flowers because their fragrance is all they have to give. Remember," she concluded, tenderly, "love is all a woman has to give," and she laid a strange, sweet accent on the all, "but it is the only thing which God permits us to carry beyond the grave."

She at last upon these promises was quiet, and very kind we were, and so to sleep, and

She attended him to excute it, but ill blood is made by it.

She bandied no more words with him, but hurried away, reaching her own door quite out of breath.

She bare also Shaaph the father of Madmannah, Sheva the father of Machbenah, and the father of Gibea: and the daughter of Caleb was Achsa.

She became a girl of considerable taste.

She became conscious of an inequality.

She became for the moment a repentant.

She became restless and dissatisfied, not exactly, as she thought, with Hurstwood, but with life.

She became the King's mistress soon after the Restoration, and was in 1670 made Baroness Nonsuch, Countess of Southampton, and Duchess of Cleveland.

She began also to think what she would have done if she had gone out into the street when she first started.

She began to be ashamed.

She began to dress at three o'clock for her departure at half-past five for the noted dining-room which was then crowding Delmonico's for position in society.

She began to feel as if the matter were in her hands entirely.

She began to feel that she had a place in the world.

She began to feel that she had made a mistake.

She began to feel that she would like to go too, and her mother agreed with her.

She began to feel the bitterness of the situation.

She began to feel the part, and summoned an indifferent smile to her lips, turning as the lines directed and going to a window, as if he were not present.

She began to gather up her poor little grip and closed her hand firmly upon her purse.

She began to get letters and cards.

She began to get the hang of those little things which the pretty woman who has vanity invariably adopts.

She began to look upon Hurstwood wholly as a man, and not as a lover or husband.

She began to pull the basket over, and now, in spite of all protest, she had swung over and was going down.

She began to read the newspaper notices, not only of the opera in which she had so small a part, but of others.

She began to see that her relations with Drouet would have to be abandoned.

She began to see that she herself had been drifting.

She began to see that they looked upon her complaint as unwarranted, and that she was supposed to work on and say nothing.

She began to step backward toward the door, when something about her plaintive face attracted him.

She began to think the world was taking note of her.

She began to wonder how one would go about getting a place.

She begins to draw very well, and I think do as well, if not better, than my wife, if it be true that she do it herself, what she shews me, and so to bed, and my head akeing all night with the wine I drank to-day, and my eyes ill.

She begins not at all to take pleasure in me or study to please.

She begins not at all to take pleasure in me or study to please.

She begins not at all to take pleasure in me or study to please.

She begun to talk in the morning and to be friends, believing all this while that.

She being gone, I fell upon boring holes for me to see from my closet into the great office, without going forth, wherein I please myself much.

She being gone I to the office, and there late doing business, and so home to supper and to bed.

She being gone, I to White Hall and there to Lord Arlington's, and met Mr. Williamson, and find there is no more need of my trouble about the Galliott, so with content departed, and went straight home, where at the office did the most at the office in that wearied and sleepy state I could, and so home to supper, and after supper falling to singing with Mercer did however sit up with her, she pleasing me with her singing of "Helpe, helpe," 'till past midnight and I not a whit drowsy, and so to bed.

She being gone, my wife and I home by coach, and then I presently by water with Mr. Pierce to Westminster Hall, he in the way telling me how the Duke of York and Duke of Albemarle do not agree.

She being gone, my wife and I to see Sir W. Pen and there supped with him much against my stomach, for the dishes were so deadly foule that I could not endure to look upon them.

She being within I left my wife there, and I to the Privy Seal, where I despatch some business, and from thence to Mrs. Blackburne again, who did treat my wife and me with a great deal of civility, and did give us a fine collation of collar of beef, &c.

She bent.

She bestowed fat pears neatly, head by tail, and among them ripe shamefaced peaches.

She big with child.

(SHE BITES HIS EAR GENTLY WITH LITTLE GOLDSTOPPED TEETH, SENDING ON HIM A CLOYING BREATH OF STALE GARLIC.

She blinked up out of her avid shameclosing eyes, mewing plaintively and long, showing him her milkwhite teeth.

She blushed, and hid her face awhile; but at last I forced her to tell me.

(SHE BLUSHES AND MAKES A KNEE)

She boarded a car in the best of spirits, feeling her blood still flowing pleasantly.

She bore his children and she laid pennies on his eyes to keep his eyelids closed when he lay on his deathbed.

She bows her old head to a voice that speaks to her loudly, her bonesetter, her medicineman: me she slights.

(SHE BREAKS OFF AND NIBBLES A PIECE GIVES A PIECE TO KITTY RICKETTS AND THEN TURNS KITTENISHLY TO LYNCH)

She breathed deeply and with delight.

She brings me luck.

She broke off suddenly.

She bronze, dealing from her oblique jar thick syrupy liquor for his lips, looked as it flowed (flower in his coat: who gave him?), and syrupped with her voice: --Fine goods in small parcels. That is to say she.

She brooded over this until she was in a state of mental rebellion.

She brought back to his recollection the happy days of blissful childhood together on the banks of Anna Liffey when they had indulged in the innocent pastimes of the young and, oblivious of the dreadful present, they both laughed heartily, all the spectators, including the venerable pastor, joining in the general merriment.

She built up feelings and a determination which the occasion did not warrant.

She buys dear and sells cheap.

She by and by in a rage follows me, and coming to me tells me in spitefull manner like a vixen and with a look full of rancour that she would go buy a new one and lace it and make me pay for it, and then let me burn it if I would after she had done it, and so went away in a fury.

She, by my Lady's advice, desires a new petticoat of the new silk striped stuff, very pretty.

She called Neale up to her, and sent for a priest, married presently, and went to bed.

She calls her children home in their dark language.

She calls the doctor sir Peter Teazle and picks buttercups off the quilt.

She calls you Solomon, and she must know, being your sister.

She came away suffering as though she had lost something.

She came bravely enough to the showy entrance way, with the polished and begilded lobby, set with framed pictures out of the current attraction, leading up to the quiet box-office, but she could get no further.

She came down from her bed, to look at him in his sleep that night.

She came faintly across the stage, saying: "And you, sir; we have been looking for you since eight o'clock," but with so little colour and in such a feeble voice that it was positively painful.

She came fresh from the air of the village, the light of the country still in her eye.

She came in and sat down at her place, feeling exceedingly wretched.

She came out feeling that luck was against her.

"She came out here," he said, looking about him, "turned this way, must have trod on these stones often."

She came out of the warm shop at six and shivered as the wind struck her.

She came to bespeak a monument for her first love, who had been killed by a whale in the Pacific ocean, no less than forty years ago.

She came to the door and looked in.

She came to thoroughly dislike the light-headed young fellows of the shop.

She came upon the corset counter and paused in rich reverie as she noted the dainty concoctions of colour and lace there displayed.

"She can afford to dress well," thought Carrie, "and so could I, if I could only keep my money. I haven't a decent tie of any kind to wear."

"She can't refuse to help me a little," he kept saying to himself.

"She can't be long, now," he said to himself, half fearing to encounter her and equally depressed at the thought that she might have gone in by another way.

She cared nothing for you.

She carried her gloves in her hand.

She carries years' water in her.

She cast about vainly for some possible place to apply, but found no door which she had the courage to enter.

She caught her little red lip with her teeth and felt her first thrill of power.

She caught up her skirts with an easy swing, for had not Drouet remarked that in her and several others, and Carrie was naturally imitative.

(SHE CLAPS HER HANDS)

She cleaned up the things one morning after he had gone, dressed as neatly as her wardrobe permitted, and set out for Broadway.

She climbed their crooked tree and I ... A saint couldn't resist it.

(SHE CLUTCHES AGAIN IN HER ROBE)

(SHE CLUTCHES THE TWO CROWNS)

She come and lay upon the bed; I up and to the office, where all the morning.

She comes very near getting drowned--no, that's not it.

She come to see us and to tell me that her husband is going to build his house again, and would borrow of me L300, which I shall upon good security be willing to do, and so told her, being willing to have some money out of my hands upon good security.

She conceived a true estimate of Drouet.

She conceived of delights which were not--saw lights of joy that never were on land or sea.

She concluded by thanking him for his kindness in a crude way, then puzzled over the formality of signing her name, and finally decided upon the severe, winding up with a "Very truly," which she subsequently changed to "Sincerely."

She concurs with me in the falseness of Sir W. Pen's friendship, and she tells pretty storms of my Lord Bruncker since he come to our end of the town, of people's applications to Mrs. Williams.

She considereth a field, and buyeth it: with the fruit of her hands she planteth a vineyard.

She could act.

She could almost see the swift answering flash of admiration in his eyes that set her tingling in every nerve.

She could also note a thing or two out of the side of her eye.

She could clearly see that this easy-going soul intended no move in her behalf.

She could do nothing but view him with gnawing contempt.

She could feel that her request disturbed him.

She could feel that there was no warm, sympathetic friendship back of the easy merriment with which many approached her.

She could find heart only to look at the pictures which were showy and then walk out.

She could formulate no thought which would be just and right.

She could get fifty dollars for those if she went to a pawnbroker.

She could get something and then work up.

She could go to Waukesha right away if she wanted to.

She could hardly believe her senses--so good-natured and tractable had he invariably been.

She could hardly keep from feeling what he felt.

She could hardly restrain herself from laughing loudly.

She could hardly tell why the one-time keen interest in him was no longer with her.

She could hardly wait until he should ask her, and yet she did not have the vanity to bring it up.

She could have laid her head upon his shoulder, so delightful did it all seem.

She could have understood the meaning of a little stone-cutter's yard at Columbia City, carving little pieces of marble for individual use, but when the yards of some huge stone corporation came into view, filled with spur tracks and flat cars, transpierced by docks from the river and traversed overhead by immense trundling cranes of wood and steel, it lost all significance in her little world.

She could look about on her gowns and carriage, her furniture and bank account.

She could never arrange her thoughts in fluent order.

She could never deliver me; I imagined that she always brought me back after showing me such things.

She could not begin to believe that she would take the place, modest as her aspirations were.

She could not buy new shoes and wear them here.

She could not, for the life of her, assume the attitude and smartness of Mrs. Vance, who, in her beauty, was all assurance.

She could not for the moment explain it, for in the next glance or the next move of the hand there was seeming indifference, mingled only with the kindest attention.

She could not get at the points that were so serious, the things she was going to make plain to him.

She could not go past them.

She could not have framed thoughts which would have expressed his defect or made clear the difference between them, but she felt it.

She could not help but feel a little choked for breath—a little sick as her heart beat so fast.

She could not help feeling, as she looked across the lovely park, that life was a joyous thing for those who did not need to worry, and she wished over and over that something might interfere now to preserve for her the comfortable state which she had occupied.

She could not help feeling pleased as she looked at herself.

She could not help feeling the claim of each trinket and valuable upon her personally, and yet she did not stop.

She could not help feeling the strangeness of her situation.

She could not help sharing in Lola's love for a good time.

She could not help smiling.

She could not help smiling as he told her of some popular actress of whom she reminded him.

She could not imagine that there would be anything in such a lofty sphere for her.

- She could not persuade herself as to the advisability of her promise, or that now, having given her word, she ought to keep it.

- She could not realize that she was drifting, until he secured her address.

- She could not repress her delight in doing this little thing which, to an ordinary observer, had no importance at all.

- She could not resist the glow of his temperament, the light of his eye.

- She could not shut out the consciousness of his individuality and presence for a moment.

- She could not understand what had gotten into the man.

- She couldn't come to-night.

- She couldn't stay.

- She could only approach that subject with a pang of sorrow and regret.

- She could only imagine that it must be evident to many that she was the less handsomely dressed of the two.

- She could only think of people connected with them as counting money, dressing magnificently, and riding in carriages.

- She could play only moderately herself, and such variety as Mrs. Vance exercised bordered, for Carrie, upon the verge of great art.

She could possibly have conquered the fear of hunger and gone back; the thought of hard work and a narrow round of suffering would, under the last pressure of conscience, have yielded, but spoil her appearance?--be old-clothed and poor-appearing?--never!

She could probably do well there.

She could scarcely force herself to answer, but managed to say "No," sharply.

She could scarcely prevent her voice from trembling.

She could scarcely toss her head gracefully.

She could scarcely answer, "I trust in you."

She could see at once by his dark eyes and his pale intellectual face that he was a foreigner, the image of the photo she had of Martin Harvey, the matinee idol, only for the moustache which she preferred because she wasn't stagestruck like Winny Rippingham that wanted they two to always dress the same on account of a play but she could not see whether he had an aquiline nose or a slightly RETROUSSE from where he was sitting.

She could see from the scrupulous care which he exercised in the matter of his personal appearance that his interest in life had abated not a jot.

She could see he wanted her, and turned to go.

She could see now that he was "broke."

She could see that Drouet did not have the keenest sensibilities.

She could see that the Hansons seldom or never had any company.

She could see them moving about now and then upon the upper floors.

She could see the tall runway and the heap of earth and coal cast out.

She could think of nothing worth while to say.

She could think of no way of explaining.

She could think of things she would like to do, of clothes she would like to wear, and of places she would like to visit.

She could without difficulty, he said, have posed for the ensemble, not to dwell on certain opulent curves of the.

She counterassaulted.

(SHE COUNTS)

She cried at my going; but whether it was at her unwillingness for my going, or any unkindness of my wife's, or no, I know not; but, God forgive me! I take her to be so cunning and ill-natured, that I have no great love for her; but only [she] is my sister, and must be provided for.

(SHE CRIES)

She crieth at the gates, at the entry of the city, at the coming in at the doors.

She crieth in the chief place of concourse, in the openings of the gates: in the city she uttereth her words, saying, How long,

ye simple ones, will ye love simplicity? and the scorners
delight in their scorning, and fools hate knowledge?

She crossed over and walked directly toward the entrance.

(SHE CROSSES THE THRESHOLD.

SHE CUFFS THEM ON, HER STREAMERS FLAUNTING
ALOFT.)

She curtseyed and went out, followed by Buck Mulligan's
tender chant:
 --HEART OF MY HEART, WERE IT MORE,
 MORE WOULD BE LAID AT YOUR FEET.

She curtseyed to him (young ladies made curtseys in those
days), with a pretty desire to convey to him that she felt
how much older and wiser he was than she.

She dances, capers, wagging her sowish haunches and her hips,
on her gross belly flapping a ruby egg.

She dances in a foul gloom where gum burns with garlic.

She dare not bear the sunnygolden babe of day.

She darted, bronze, to the backmost corner, flattening her face
against the pane in a halo of hurried breath.

(SHE DARTS BACK TO THE TABLE)

(SHE DARTS TO THE PIANO AND BANGS CHORDS ON
IT WITH CROSSED ARMS)

She dawned upon the audience, handsome and proud, shifting, with the necessity of the situation, to a cold, white, helpless object, as the social pack moved away from her scornfully.

She decided to stop in at the Madison Square Theatre and ask how to find the theatrical agents.

She decided to take up that opportunity on the morrow.

She desired I would take a good time and manner of proposing it, and I said I would, though I believed he would love nothing but money, and much was not to be expected there, she said.

She'd have won the money only for the other dog.

She did.

She did act sort of funny at times.

She did get flushed in the wind.

She did give him a cold answer, but not so severe as it ought to have been; and, it seems, as the lady since to my Lady confesses, he had wrote a letter to her, which she answered slightly, and was resolved to contemn any motion of his therein.

She did give me account of this wedding to-day, its being private being imputed to its being just before Lent, and so in vain to make new clothes till Easter, that they might see the fashions as they are like to be this summer; which is reason good enough.

She did give me an account of great differences between her mother and Balty's wife.

She did, indeed, start.

She did it because it was pleasant and a relief from dulness of the home over which her husband brooded.

She did it up all by herself and what joy was hers when she tried it on then, smiling at the lovely reflection which the mirror gave back to her!

She did it with a grace which was fascinating to look upon.

She did live last at my Lord Monk's house, and indeed at dinner did get what there was very prettily ready and neat for me, which did please me much.

She did look so nice.

She did manage to inquire at the box-office, however.

She did not answer.

She did not blame Minnie, she did not blame Hanson very much.

She did not credit her willingness to go to any fascination Hurstwood held for her.

She did not do the part as she had at rehearsal, but she was better.

She did not explain that the thought, however, had aroused all the antagonism of her nature.

She did not feel herself defeated at all.

She did not forget her own difficult struggle in Chicago, but she did not forget either that she had never ceased trying.

She did not fully realise that this was so, but there was something in condescension coming from her which was infinitely sweet.

She did not greatly alter in appearance.

She did not grow in knowledge so much as she awakened in the matter of desire.

She did not hear this very well.

She did not know exactly what she would do or how she would explain to Drouet, if he came.

She did not know just how such applications were made, but she took it to be a matter which related more directly to the theatre buildings.

She did not know that the girl was dead.

She did not know that thoroughfare very well.

She did not know what to think.

She did not know whether she would ever see this man any more.

She did not look about.

She did not look well enough.

She did not mind.

She did not move her eyes from the flat, open scene before her.

She did not need to tremble at all, because it was invisible; she did not need to worry over what other people would say--what she herself would say--because it had no tangibility.

She did not propose to be quarrelled with.

She did not realise this at first, being affected by some of the old distress which was a result of her earlier adventure into this strenuous and exacting quarter.

She did not recover.

She did not run away, as she might have done.

She did not seem to feel that he was wretched.

She did not study him with eyes expressive of dependence.

She did not suggest to Hurstwood that he come and see.

She did not take into account how much liberty she was securing.

She did not terminate the interview, but she drifted off into a pleasant field of thought with the readiest grace.

She did not try to conjecture what the drift of the conversation would be.

She did not venture to look around, but above the clack of the machine she could hear an occasional remark.

She did not want anything to do with him.

She did not want Drouet or his money when she thought of it, nor anything more to do with Hurstwood, but only the content and ease of mind she had experienced, for, after all, she had been happy--happier, at least, than she was now when confronted by the necessity of making her way alone.

She did not want to borrow of Minnie for that.

She did not want to go in yet a while.

She did not want to make any one who had been good to her feel badly.

She did not wholly believe that he would, but he might.

She did not see Ames any more.

She did not quarrel now with Hurstwood's idleness.

She did not realise what she was doing by allowing these feelings to possess her.

She didn't deserve what she got out of me, that is sure.

She didn't know exactly what to answer.

SHE DIDN'T KNOW WHAT TO DO
TO KEEP IT UP
TO KEEP IT UP.

She didn't like her plate full.

She didn't like it because I sprained my ankle first day she wore choir picnic at the Sugarloaf.

She didn't mean it, Mr Bello.

She didn't say a word to me.

She didn't want anything.

She did, of course, the cat!

She died 1686.

She died at their house in Crutched Friars, and was buried at St. Olave's Church, Hart Street, where Pepys erected a monument to her memory.

She died December 31st, 1705.

She died, for literature at least, before she was born.

She died January 15th, 1757, at ninety-six years, four months.

She died January 27th, 1721-22, aged eighty-four.

She died July, 1665 (see "Memoires de Grammont," chap. viii.).

She died October 9th, 1709, aged sixty-nine.

She died, Stephen retorted, sixtyseven years after she was born.

(SHE DIES)

She dined with me; and after dinner I took coach, and carried her home; in our way, in Cheapside, lighting and giving her a dozen pair of white gloves as my Valentine.

She dined with me, my wife being ill of her months in bed.

She dined with us, and after dinner went away again, being agreed to come to us about three weeks or a month hence.

She disliked to listen to the girl next to her, who was rather hardened by experience.

She disliked umbrella with rain, he liked woman with umbrella, she disliked new hat with rain, he liked woman with new hat, he bought new hat with rain, she carried umbrella with new hat.

She distinguished very carefully between the young boys of the school, many of whom were attracted by her beauty.

She'd like scent of that kind.

She'd never make an actress, though.

"She doesn't mind," answered Jessica, coolly.

She doesn't notice a word!

She does whack it, by George.

She do protest, before God, she never did see the account, but that it was as her husband in his life-time made it, and he did often declare to her his expecting L500, and that we could not deny it him for his pains in that business, and that he hath left her worth nothing of his own in the world, and that therefore she could pay nothing of it, come what will come, but that he hath left her a beggar, which I am sorry truly for, though it is a just judgment upon people that do live so much beyond themselves in housekeeping and vanity, as they did.

She doted upon the Assyrians her neighbours, captains and rulers clothed most gorgeously, horsemen riding upon horses, all of them desirable young men.

She do tell me that this child did come is 'meme jour that it ought to hazer after my avoir ete con elle before her marid did venir home . . . . Thence to the Swan, and there I sent for Sarah, and mighty merry we were . . . . So to Sir Robert Viner's about my plate, and carried home another dozen of plates, which makes my stock of plates up 2 1/2 dozen, and at home find Mr. Thomas Andrews, with whom I staid and talked a little and invited him to dine with me at Christmas, and then I to the office, and there late doing business, and so home and to bed.

She doubled a slice of bread into her mouth, asking: --What time is the funeral?

She doubted the naturalness of so large a bill.

(SHE DRAWS A PONIARD AND, CLAD IN THE SHEATHMAIL OF AN ELECTED KNIGHT OF NINE, STRIKES AT HIS LOINS)

SHE DRAWS FROM BEHIND, OGLING, AND SHOWS COYLY HER BLOODIED CLOUT.)

She dressed herself in a worn shirt-waist of dotted blue percale, a skirt of light-brown serge rather faded, and a small straw hat which she had worn all summer at Columbia City.

She drew closer to him, and kissed his cheek and his hand.

She drew down pensive (why did he go so quick when I?) about her bronze, over the bar where bald stood by sister gold, inexquisite contrast, contrast inexquisite nonexquisite, slow cool dim seagreen sliding depth of shadow, EAU DE NIL.

She drew herself up to her full height.

She drew to herself commendation from her two admirers which she had not earned.

(SHE DROPS TWO PENNIES IN THE SLOT.

She drove out more, dressed better, and attended theatres freely to make up for it.

She dwelleth and abideth on the rock, upon the crag of the rock, and the strong place.

She encountered a very similar experience in the office of Mr. Jenks, only he varied it by saying at the close: "If you could play at some local house, or had a programme with your name on it, I might do something."

She endeavoured to stir, but it was useless.

She ended all with a promise of shells to my wife, very fine ones indeed, and seems to have great respect and honour for my wife.

Sheep of the prisons, emissary of Republican committees, now turnkey, now prisoner, always spy and secret informer, so much the more valuable here for being English that an Englishman is less open to suspicion of subornation in those characters than a Frenchman, represents himself to his employers under a false name.

Sheep was a cant word of the time for a spy, under the gaolers.

Sheer force of natural genius, that.

Sheet kindly lent.

Sheet lightning courage.

Sheet of her music blew out of my hand against the High school railings.

She even answered for a waitress in a small restaurant where she saw a card in the window, but they wanted an experienced girl.

(SHE FADES FROM HIS SIDE.

She faintly shook her head upon the pillow, and kept her secret, as the boy had done.

She fancied she and Carrie were somewhere beside an old coal-mine.

She feared that she would forget her lines, that she might be unable to master the feeling which she now felt concerning her own movements in the play.

She feared that the young boys about would address such remarks to her--boys who, beside Drouet, seemed uncouth and ridiculous.

She felt abashed at the man's daring, but could only smile in answer to his engaging smirk, and say: "I need to make a living."

She felt a kind of a sensation rushing all over her and she knew by the feel of her scalp and that irritation against her stays that that thing must be coming on because the last time too was when she clipped her hair on account of the moon.

She felt a little older than they.

She felt a little out of place, but the great room soothed her and the view of the well-dressed throng outside seemed a splendid thing.

She felt ashamed.

She felt ashamed in part because she had been weak enough to take it, but her need was so dire, she was still glad.

She felt ashamed in the face of better dressed girls who went by.

She felt as if hard thoughts were unjust.

She felt as if she ought to continue and inquire elsewhere, but the results so far were too dispiriting.

She felt as if she would like to be agreeable to this young man, and also there came with it, or perhaps preceded it, the slightest shade of a feeling that he was better educated than she was--that his mind was better.

She felt as if the thing deserved an answer, and consequently decided that she would write and let him know that she knew of his married state and was justly incensed at his deception.

She felt a slight relief, but it was only at her escape.

She felt, as the minutes passed, that the room was not very light.

She felt as though she could hardly endure such a life.

She felt as though she should be better served, and her heart revolted.

She felt at times as if she could cry out and make such a row that some one would come to her aid; at other times it seemed an almost useless thing--so far was she from any aid, no matter what she did.

She felt a wave of feeling sweep over her at this.

She felt bound to him by a strange tie of affection now.

She felt him observing her mass of hair.

She felt his admiration.

She felt his drawing toward her in every sound of his voice.

She felt his indifference keenly and longed to see Hurstwood.

She felt Hurstwood's passion as a delightful background to her own achievement, and she wondered what he would have to say.

She felt mildly guilty of something--perhaps unworthiness.

She felt more than ever the helplessness of her case.

She felt now was the time to express to Carrie the state of Hanson's feeling about her entire Chicago venture.

She felt rather sorry for him--a sorrow born of what had only recently been a great admiration.

She felt something lost to her when he moved away.

She felt so relieved in his radiant presence, so much looked after and cared for, that she assented gladly, though with the slightest air of holding back.

She felt so thrilled that she must needs walk back to the hotel to think, wondering what she should do.

She felt that he considered she was doing a great deal.

She felt that her life was becoming stale, and therein she felt cause for gloom.

She felt that he was good to speak as he had, although it did not concern her at all. She did not know why she felt this way.

She felt that she could do things if she only had a chance.

She felt that she liked him—that she could continue to like him ever so much.

She felt that she was more clever with him than with others.

She felt that she was so obscure it did not matter.

She felt that the drummer had injured her irreparably.

She felt that the man was gentle, and that his interest in her had not abated, and it made her suffer a pang of regret.

She felt the acuteness of Hurstwood's position, and wished deeply that she could be alone with him, but she did not understand the change in Drouet.

She felt the drag of a lean and narrow life.

She felt the eyes of the other help upon her, and troubled lest she was not working fast enough.

She felt the flood of feeling.

She felt the flow of the tide of effort and interest--felt her own helplessness without quite realising the wisp on the tide that she was.

She felt the need of a breath of fresh air and a drink of water, but did not venture to stir.

She felt the strain of publicity.

She felt the warm flush, a danger signal always with Gerty MacDowell, surging and flaming into her cheeks.

She felt the worn state of her shoes.

She felt thoroughly bound to him as a wife, and that her lot was cast with his, whatever it might be; but she began to see that he was gloomy and taciturn, not a young, strong, and buoyant man.

She felt, though she seldom expressed them, sad thoughts upon this score.

She felt very much like a criminal in the matter.

She figured the possibilities in such cases.

She finds that I am lousy.

She finds that I am lousy.

She finds that I am lousy.

SHE FIXES HER BLUECIRCLED HOLLOW EYESOCKETS ON STEPHEN AND OPENS HER TOOTHLESS MOUTH UTTERING A SILENT WORD.

She folded the card into her untidy bag and snapped the catch.

She followed not all, a part of the whole, gave attention with interest comprehended with surprise, with care repeated, with greater difficulty remembered, forgot with ease, with misgiving reremembered, rerepeated with error.

She followed him diffidently through the clattering automatons, keeping her eyes straight before her, and flushing slightly.

She followed whither her craving led.

She follows her mother with ungainly steps, a mare leading her fillyfoal.

She forgot her youth and her beauty.

She forgot, in part, and was merry.

She forgot that if she were alone she would have to pay for a room and board, and imagined that every cent of her eighteen could be spent for clothes and things that she liked.

She found, after all--as what millionaire has not?—that there was no realising, in consciousness, the meaning of large sums.

She found, after a time, that her back was beginning to ache.

She foundered in the sea.

She found herself asking him questions about little things.

She found him lifting her head and looking into her eyes.

She found it was not such a wonderful thing to be in the chorus, and she also learned that her salary would be twelve dollars a week.

She found there was no discrimination between one and the other of applicants, save as regards a conventional standard of prettiness and form.

She freed from her father-in-law's tyranny, and is in condition to helpe her mother, who needs it; of which I am glad, the young lady being very pretty.

(SHE FREES HERSELF, DROOPS ON A CHAIR.

She frowned and frowned, but to no effect.

(SHE FROWNS WITH LOWERED HEAD)

She fulfilled her household duties and said little to disturb him.

She fumbled her purse which contained the address slip.

She gained some inkling of the character of Hanson's life when, half asleep, she looked out into the dining-room at six o'clock and saw him silently finishing his breakfast.

She gave her moist (a lady's) hand to his firm clasp.

She gave him credit for having the usual allurements of men-- people to talk to, places to stop, friends to consult with.

She gave him credit for his good looks, his generous feelings, and even, in fact, failed to recollect his egotism when he was absent; but she could not feel any binding influence keeping her for him as against all others.

She gave vent to her opinions in the kitchen where the cook was.

She gazed and gazed, wondering, delighting, longing, and all the while the siren voice of the unrestful was whispering in her ear.

She gazed at him--a pythoness in humour.

She gazed at the green landscape, now passing in swift review until her swifter thoughts replaced its impression with vague conjectures of what Chicago might be.

She gazed into the lighted street when Minnie brought her into the front room, and wondered at the sounds, the movement, the murmur of the vast city which stretched for miles and miles in every direction.

She gazed out towards the distant sea.

She gazed straight before her, inhaling through her arched nostrils.

She gazed weakly at him and said: "Well, what do you think you will do? A hundred dollars won't last long."

She gets you a job on the paper and then you go and slate her drivel to Jaysus.

She girdeth her loins with strength, and strengtheneth her arms.

(SHE GIVES HIM THE GLAD EYE)

She glanced at him as she bent forward quickly, a pathetic little glance of piteous protest, of shy reproach under which he coloured like a girl He was leaning back against the rock behind.

(SHE GLANCES BACK)

(SHE GLANCES ROUND HER AT THE COUPLES.

(SHE GLIDES AWAY CROOKEDLY.

SHE GLIDES SIDLING AND BOWING, TWIRLING JAPANESILY.)

She goes next before him--is gone; the knitting-women count Twenty-Two.

(SHE GOES TO THE CHANDELIER AND TURNS THE GAS FULL COCK)

(SHE GOES TO THE PIANOLA.

She goes to window.

She gone, Creed and I to the King's playhouse, and saw an act or two of the new play ["Evening's Love"] again, but like it not.

She gone, I by coach home, and there busy at my letters till night, and then with my wife in the evening singing with her in the garden with great pleasure, and so home to supper and to bed.

She gone I late at my business, and then home to supper and to bed.

She gone, I to bed.

She gone, I to my business and did much, and among other
   things to-night we were all mightily troubled how to
   prevent the sale of a great deal of hemp, and timber-deals,
   and other good goods to-morrow at the candle by the Prize
   Office, where it will be sold for little, and we shall be found
   to want the same goods and buy at extraordinary prices,
   and perhaps the very same goods now sold, which is a most
   horrid evil and a shame.

She gone, I to my very great content do find my accounts to
   come very even and naturally, and so to supper and to bed.

She gone I to other business in my chamber, and then to supper
   and to bed.

She gone, I to supper, and then to read a little, and to bed.

She gone, I up and then hear that my wife and her maid Ashwell
   had between them spilled the pot . . . . upon the floor and
   stool and God knows what, and were mighty merry making
   of it clean.

She gone I went to see Mrs. Jem, at whose chamber door
   I found a couple of ladies, but she not being there, we
   hunted her out, and found that she and another had hid
   themselves behind a door.

She gone, we to bed all.

She got a pretty letter from the manager, saying that by the time
   she got it he would be waiting for her in the park.

She got ninepence of me.

She got the location of several playhouses fixed in her mind--notably the Grand Opera House and McVickar's, both of which were leading in attractions--and then came away.

She got the things, she said.

She grows mighty homely and looks old.

She had.

She had a chic way of tossing her head to one side, and holding her arms as if for action--not listlessly.

She had a gorgeous, simply gorgeous, time.

She had a line presently which was supposed to be funny.

She had a little time at least, and then, perhaps, everything would come out all right, after all.

She had also about forty good brass guns, but will make little amends to our loss in The Prince.

She had amused herself with a walk, a book by Bertha M. Clay which Drouet had left there, though she did not wholly enjoy the latter, and by changing her dress for the evening.

She had an ideal to contrast men by--particularly men close to her.

She had a place--she had a place!

She had applied in the cheapest kind of places without success.

She had become familiar to me, when a gracious God restored my faculties; but, I am quite unable even to say how she had become familiar.

She had been astonishingly persistent.

She had been dominated by distress and the enthusiastic forces of relief which Drouet represented at an opportune moment when she yielded to him.

She had been regretting the wane of a pleasant evening, but she had thought there was a half-hour more.

She had been taught how to dress and where to go without having ample means to do either.

She had been troubled in a way by doubt and longing, but these had made no deeper impression than could be traced in a certain open wistfulness of glance and speech.

She had been used to better than that.

She had believed it was all legal and binding enough.

She had cause to ponder over this until they met again—several weeks or more.

She had come down to the breakfast table feeling a little out of sorts with herself and revolving a scheme which she had in her mind.

She had come upon it as one who stumbles upon a secret passage and, behold, she was in the chamber of diamonds and delight!

- She had come up the imposing steps, guarded by the large and portly doorman.

- She had constantly had her attention called by the latter to novelties in everything which pertains to a woman's apparel.

- She had cut it that very morning on account of the new moon and it nestled about her pretty head in a profusion of luxuriant clusters and pared her nails too, Thursday for wealth.

- She had dimly heard of these things, but it seemed strange to be called to order from the list.

- She had done sitting the first time, and indeed her face is mighty like at first dash.

- She had done something which was above his sphere.

- She had drawn close to him, in her dread of the scene, and in her pity for the prisoner.

- She had employed herself in both ways, at his side under the tree, many and many a time; but, this time was not quite like any other, and nothing could make it so.

- She had enjoyed Mrs. Vance's companionship so much.

- She had enough of the instincts of a housewife to take great satisfaction in these things.

- She had expected that it would be more difficult, that something cold and harsh would be said--she knew not what.

- She had felt it all the time.

She had forgotten, in considering and explaining the result of her day, that Drouet might come.

She had fought the good fight and now she was very very happy.

She had found the company so nervous that her own strength had gone.

She had four dinky sets with awfully pretty stitchery, three garments and nighties extra, and each set slotted with different coloured ribbons, rosepink, pale blue, mauve and peagreen, and she aired them herself and blued them when they came home from the wash and ironed them and she had a brickbat to keep the iron on because she wouldn't trust those washerwomen as far as she'd see them scorching the things.

She had gone willingly to seek him, with sympathy in her heart, when Hurstwood had reported him ill.

She had got and used some puppy-dog water.

She had got and used some puppy-dog water.

She had got and used some puppy-dog water.

She had had a dreary day of it herself.

She had had no experience with this class of individuals whatsoever, and did not know the salacity and humour of the theatrical tribe.

She had had nothing to eat, and yet there she sat, thinking it over.

She had had no word from any quarter, she had spent a dollar of her precious sum in procuring food and paying car fare.

She had heard it spoken of as having a splendid restaurant.

She had heard of the Hudson River, the great city of New York, and now she looked out, filling her mind with the wonder of it.

She had heard Parson Herring take his leave; tho' he, by reading so much of the Common Prayer as he did, hath cast himself out of the good opinion of both sides.

She had heard so much of the canting philosophy of the grapeless fox.

She had her elbow in an awkward position under her side.

She had here one picture upon the top, with these words, dedicating it to the memory of her husband: --"Incomparabili marito, inconsolabilis vidua."

She had her hand out on the table before her.

She had imagination enough to be moody.

She had in part suspected, and in part discovered, the main facts of the cruel story, of her husband's share in it, and my being resorted to.

She had installed herself, some time before, as Mr. Lorry's cup-bearer; and while they sat under the plane-tree, talking, she kept his glass replenished.

She had interrogated constantly at varying intervals as to the correct method of writing the capital initial of the name of a city in Canada, Quebec.

She had invited Carrie, not because she longed for her presence, but because the latter was dissatisfied at home, and could probably get work and pay her board here.

She had just recently donned a sailor hat for the season with a band of pretty white-dotted blue silk.

She had laid her head upon my shoulder, that night when I was summoned out--she had a fear of my going, though I had none--and when I was brought to the North Tower they found these upon my sleeve.

She had learned much about laces and those little neckpieces which add so much to a woman's appearance.

She had learned that in his world, as in her own present state, was not happiness.

She had learned that men could change and fail.

She had listened to Drouet's enthusiastic maunderings with much regard for that part which concerned herself, with very little for that which affected his own gain.

She had looked back at times upon her parting from Drouet and had regretted that she had served him so badly.

She had loved him better than he knew.

She had loved his weak watery blood drained from her own.

- She had marvelled at the insistence and superior airs of Mr. Millice, but the individual conducting here had the same insistence, coupled with almost brutal roughness.

- She had moved from the wall of the garret, very near to the bench on which he sat.

- She had nestled down with him, that his head might lie upon her arm; and her hair drooping over him curtained him from the light.

- She had never been on the road.

- She had never been quite at her ease with him, and received him with some little embarrassment as he seated himself near her table.

- She had never come in contact with such grace.

- She had never done this thing before, and lacked courage.

- She had never forgotten her one histrionic achievement in Chicago.

- She had never seen him softened, and was much distressed.

- She had never seen such a little flat as hers, and yet it soon enlisted her affection.

- She had never thought of him in connection with money troubles before.

- She had no fear of his striking at her with the knife, though they had.

- She had no idea what Hurstwood's next word would be.

She had no idea what it meant or that it was important.

She had no intention of being at their beck and call.

She had no navel.

She had none laid up for such an emergency.

She had no particular regard for Carrie, whom she took to be cold and disagreeable.

She had no sooner entered the flat than this point was settled for her.

She had no special evidence wherewith to justify herself-- the knowledge of something which would give her both authority and excuse.

She had not been able to get away this morning.

She had not been married many weeks, when that man's brother saw her and admired her, and asked that man to lend her to him--for what are husbands among us!

She had not expected that he would offer her less than six.

She had not failed to notice that he did not seem to consult her about buying clothes for himself.

She had not had adulation and affectionate propositions before.

She had not had fame or money before.

She had no time to look about, and bent anxiously to her task.

She had no time to lose, but must get ready at once.

She had not known of it, and it took her breath.

She had not lived, could not lay claim to having lived, until something of this had come into her own life.

She had no water, it appears, in her hold.

She had no winter jacket, no hat, no shoes.

She hadn't acted that way.

She had on a white dusting cap, beneath which her chubby face shone good-naturedly.

She had on her best, but there was comfort in the thought that if she must confine herself to a best, it was neat and fitting.

She had out her hat and gloves, and was fastening a white lace tie about her throat when the housemaid brought up the information that Mr. Hurstwood wished to see her.

She had outlived him.

She had plenty of game in her then.

She had practised her make-up in the morning, had rehearsed and arranged her material for the evening by one o'clock, and had gone home to have a final look at her part, waiting for the evening to come.

She had reached home early and went in the front room to think.

She had realised with the lapse of the quarter hours that Drouet was not coming, and somehow she felt a little resentful, a little as if she had been forsaken--was not good enough.

She had reasons for believing that there was a young sister
  living, and her greatest desire was, to help that sister.

She had recovered herself sufficiently to wish to know more of
  the details.

She had red slippers on.

She had reserved this last evening for her father, and they sat
  alone under the plane-tree.

She had risen, and now walked angrily out of the room.

She had saved him from being trampled underfoot and had
  gone, scarcely having been.

She had secured her hat and jacket and slipped the latter on
  over her little evening dress.

She had seen a number of people in her life who reminded her
  of what she had vaguely come to think of as scholars.

She had seen comparatively little of the manager during the
  winter, but had been kept constantly in mind of him by one
  thing and another, principally by the strong impression he
  had made.

She had seen notices of dances, parties, balls, and suppers at
  Sherry's.

She had seen the houses, as she came along, decorated with
  little pikes, and with little red caps stuck upon them; also,
  with tricoloured ribbons; also, with the standard inscription
  (tricoloured letters were the favourite), Republic One and
  Indivisible.

She had seen the lobby, guarded by another large and portly
    gentleman, and been waited upon by uniformed youths
    who took care of canes, overcoats, and the like.

She had six children by the King.

She had six children by the King.

She had six children by the King.

She had six children by the King, one of them being created
    Duke of Grafton, and the eldest son succeeding her as
    Duke of Cleveland.

She had some faint hopes that his mediation might save
    Charles, but they were very slight.

She had some jewelry--a diamond ring and pin and several
    other pieces.

She had some money or something and they wanted to get it.

She had some power of initiative, latent before, which now
    began to exert itself.

She had some slight gift of observation and that sense, so rich in
    every woman—intuition.

She had such a small part.

She had talked so much about getting more salary and
    confessed to so much anxiety about her future, that now,
    when the direct question of fact was waiting, she could not
    tell this girl.

She had that cream gown on with the rip she never stitched.

She had the aptitude of the struggler who seeks emancipation.

She had the cunning to cry a great while, and talk and blubber.

She had the cunning to cry a great while, and talk and blubber.

She had the cunning to cry a great while, and talk and blubber.

She had the kindliest feelings for him in every way.

She had time for some lone wanderings, but mostly he filled her hours with sight-seeing.

She had to go but they would meet again, there, and she would dream of that till then, tomorrow, of her dream of yester eve.

She had too little faith in mankind not to know that they were erring.

She had vain imaginings about place and power, about far-off lands and magnificent people.

She had wondered at the greatness of the names upon the billboards, the marvel of the long notices in the papers, the beauty of the dresses upon the stage, the atmosphere of carriages, flowers, refinement.

She half closed her eyes and tried to think it was nothing, that Columbia City was only a little way off.

She half smiled at him wanly, a sweet forgiving smile, a smile that verged on tears, and then they parted.

She hardly explained to herself why this latest invitation appealed to her most

She hardly heard anything more, save her own rumbling blood.

She hardly knew how to answer this, and yet her wrath was not placated.

She hardly knew how to continue the inquiry.

SHE HAS A BUCKET ON THE CROOK OF HER ARM AND A SCOURINGBRUSH IN HER HAND.)

"She has a fine head for it," croaked Jacques Three.

She has a fine pair, God bless her.

She has a "GAM," a thing so utterly unknown to all other ships that they never heard of the name even; and if by chance they should hear of it, they only grin at it, and repeat gamesome stuff about "spouters" and "blubber-boilers," and such like pretty exclamations.

She has a good job if she minds it till Johnny comes marching home again.

She has a husband, a father, and a brother?

She has a whole lake's contents bottled in her ample hold.

SHE HAS A SPROUTING MOUSTACHE.

She has explored seas and archipelagoes which had no chart, where no Cook or Vancouver had ever sailed.

She has gone out on some household matters, but will soon be home.

She has it.

SHE HAS IT, SHE GOT IT,
WHEREVER SHE PUT IT,
THE LEG OF THE DUCK.

SHE HAS LARGE PENDANT BERYL EARDROPS.)

She hasn't any claims on me.

She hasn't been anything for years or I wouldn't have ever come near you.

She has put into the small, unwise head of the chipmunk the untutored fear of poisons.

She has some recent association with the number twelve?

She has something to put in them.

She has such a strong attachment to you and reliance on you.

She hastened around to the side entrance and was taken up by the elevator to the fourth floor.

"She has that property in her name," he kept saying to himself.

She has the Spanish type.

She has this silly vanity that she must play.

She has this silly vanity that she must play.

She has this silly vanity that she must play.

She hated to think of going back there each evening.

She hath done what she could: she is come aforehand to anoint my body to the burying.

She hath got her teeth new done by La Roche.

She hath got her teeth new done by La Roche.

She hath got her teeth new done by La Roche.

She hath killed her beasts; she hath mingled her wine; she hath also furnished her table.

She hath sent forth her maidens: she crieth upon the highest places of the city, Whoso is simple, let him turn in hither: as for him that wanteth understanding, she saith to him, Come, eat of my bread, and drink of the wine which I have mingled.

She hath wearied herself with lies, and her great scum went not forth out of her: her scum shall be in the fire.

She hath we conceive wrought a little too much, having neither maid nor girle to help her.

(SHE HAULS UP A REEF OF HER SLIP, REVEALING HER BARE THIGH, AND UNROLLS THE POTATO FROM THE TOP OF HER STOCKING)

(SHE HAULS UP A REEF OF SKIRT AND RANSACKS THE POUCH OF HER STRIPED BLAY PETTICOAT.

She--have you seen her, Doctor?

She heard Carrie say that Hurstwood was not coming home to dinner.

She heard him open the top of the wardrobe and take out his hat.

She heard me, and ran in.

She heard old Royce sing in the pantomime of TURKO THE TERRIBLE and laughed with others when he sang:
I AM THE BOY
THAT CAN ENJOY
INVISIBILITY.

She heard some one called.

She held him closer round the neck, and rocked him on her breast like a child.

She held it to her own.

She hesitated a moment, then entered.

(SHE HICCUPS, THEN BENDS QUICKLY HER SAILOR HAT UNDER WHICH HER HAIR GLOWS, RED WITH HENNA)

SHE HOLDS A SCOTTISH WIDOWS' INSURANCE POLICY AND A LARGE MARQUEE UMBRELLA UNDER WHICH HER BROOD RUN WITH HER, PATSY HOPPING ON ONE SHOD FOOT, HIS COLLAR LOOSE, A HANK OF PORKSTEAKS DANGLING, FREDDY WHIMPERING, SUSY WITH A CRYING COD'S MOUTH, ALICE STRUGGLING WITH THE BABY.

She holds her complexion still, but in everything else, even in this her new house and the best rooms in it, and her closet which her husband with some vainglory took me to show me, she continues the eeriest slattern that ever I knew in my life.

(SHE HOLDS HIS HAND WHICH IS FEELING FOR HER NIPPLE)

She home, and I to Sir G. Carteret's about business, and so home too, and Sarah having her fit we went to bed.

She hoped she would never meet him again, but she was ashamed of her conduct.

She hummed and hummed as the moments went by, sitting in the shadow by the window, and was therein as happy, though she did not perceive it, as she ever would be.

She hung about the stove, suffered a chattering chill, and went to bed sick.

She hung at the wing's edge, wrapt in her own mounting thoughts.

She hung in doubt about this until the dinner was over.

She hunted out an unassuming restaurant and entered, but was disturbed to find that the prices were exorbitant for the size of her purse.

She hurried at her toilet, which was soon made, and hastened down the stairs.

She hurried on, tired perhaps, but no longer weary of foot.

She hurries out.

She hurries to him, and they go on together, walking up and down, walking up and down, until he is composed.

She, impending disaster itself, walked about with gathered shadow at the eyes and the rudimentary muscles of savagery fixing the hard lines of her mouth.

She in bed but pretty well, and having a messenger from my brother, that he is not well nor stirs out of doors, I went forth to see him, and found him below, he has not been well, but is not ill.

She increased in value in his eyes because of her objection.

She in love, and he hath got her to promise him to marry, and he is now cold in it, so that I must rid my hands of them, which troubles me, and the more because my head is now busy upon other greater things.

She imagined that across these richly carved entrance-ways, where the globed and crystalled lamps shone upon panelled doors set with stained and designed panes of glass, was neither care nor unsatisfied desire.

She instinctively felt that he was stronger and higher, and yet withal so simple.

She intends to force them to take their money again, and release her husband of those hard terms.

She in this sad condition took no notice of me, nor I of her.

She invariably asked her to stay, proposing little outings and other things of that sort until Carrie began neglecting her dinner hours.

She is.

She is a bad merchant.

She is afeard that my Lady Castlemaine will keep still with the King, and I am afeard she will not, for I love her well.

She is a fine confident lady, I think, but not so pretty as I once thought her.

She is a hoary pandemonium of ills, enlarged glands, mumps, quinsy, bunions, hayfever, bedsores, ringworm, floating kidney, Derbyshire neck, warts, bilious attacks, gallstones, cold feet, varicose veins.

She is a little plain woman, a Dane: her name, Ursula Dyan; about forty years old; her voice like a little girl's; with a beard as much as any man I ever saw, black almost, and grizly; they offered to shew my wife further satisfaction if she desired it, refusing it to men that desired it there, but there is no doubt but by her voice she is a woman; it begun to grow at about seven years old, and was shaved not above seven months ago, and is now so big as any man's almost that ever I saw; I say, bushy and thick.

She is a mighty proper maid, and pretty comely, but so so; but hath a most pleasing tone of voice, and speaks handsomely, but hath most great hands, and I believe ugly; but very well dressed, and good clothes, and the maid I believe will please me well enough.

She is an Angel!

She is, at least seems, in mighty trouble for her husband at sea, when I am sure she cares not for him, and I would not undeceive her, though I know his ship is one of those that is not gone, but left behind without men.

She is a tree of life to them that lay hold upon her: and happy is every one that retaineth her.

She is a very fine woman, and what with her person and the number of fine ladies that were with her, I was much out of countenance, and could hardly carry myself like a man among them; but however, I staid till my courage was up again, and talked to them, and viewed her house, which is most pleasant, and so drank and good-night.

She is a very good companion as long as she is well.

She is a very good companion as long as she is well.

She is a very good companion as long as she is well.

She is ballasted with utilities; not altogether with unusable pig-lead and kentledge.

She is coated with quite a considerable layer of fat.

She is come to put out her sister and brothers to school at Putney.

She is conceited that she do well already.

She is conceited that she do well already.

She is conceited that she do well already.

"'She is dead,' said I."

SHE IS DRESSED IN A THREEQUARTER IVORY GOWN, FRINGED ROUND THE HEM WITH TASSELLED SELVEDGE, AND COOLS HERSELF FLIRTING A BLACK HORN FAN LIKE MINNIE HAUCK IN Carmen.

She is drowning.

She is either a very prodigal woman, or richer than she would be thought, by her buying of the best things, and laying out much money in new-fashioned pewter; and, among other things, a new-fashioned case for a pair of snuffers, which is very pretty; but I could never have guessed what it was for, had I not seen the snuffers in it.

She is empty, and void, and waste: and the heart melteth, and the knees smite together, and much pain is in all loins, and the faces of them all gather blackness.

She is everything to me; more to me than suffering, more to me than wrong, more to me--Well!

She is five years younger than I, and she lives in a farmer's house in the south country.

She is frequently mentioned in the "Memoires de Grammont," and in the letters of the second Earl of Chesterfield.

She is going to be married.

She is going to lodgings, and do tell me very odde stories how Mrs. Williams do receive the applications of people, and hath presents, and she is the hand that receives all, while my Lord Bruncker do the business, which will shortly come to be loud talk if she continues here, I do foresee, and bring my Lord no great credit.

She is gone abroad with him to-day, very fine.

She is gone yesterday with her Lord to Cobham.

She is greatly distressed; but her father is comforting her, and she feels the better for being out of court.

She is great with child, and she says I must be godfather, but I do not intend it.

She is grown tall, but looks very white and thin, and I can find no occasion while I am here to come to have her company, which I desire and expected in my coming, but only coming out of the church I kissed her and her sister and mother-in-law.

She is hardened against her young ones, as though they were not her's: her labour is in vain without fear; Because God hath deprived her of wisdom, neither hath he imparted to her understanding.

She is indeed black, and hath good black little eyes, but otherwise but a very ordinary woman I do think, but they say sings well.

She is, it seems, very near akin to the King: Such mad doings there are every day among them!

She is like the merchants' ships; she bringeth her food from afar.

(She is loud and stubborn; her feet abide not in her house: Now is she without, now in the streets, and lieth in wait at every corner.)

She is more precious than rubies: and all the things thou canst desire are not to be compared unto her.

She is more taking then.

She is my sister, Doctor.

She is not afraid of the snow for her household: for all her household are clothed with scarlet.

She is not overhandsome, though a good lady, and one I love.

She is not the filly that she was.

She is now at a Taverne and stays all night, so I was obliged to give him my house and chamber to lie in, which he with great modesty and after much force took, and so I got Mr. Evelyn's coach to carry her thither, and the coach coming back, I with Mr. Evelyn to Deptford, where a little while with him doing a little business, and so in his coach back again to my lodgings, and there sat with Mrs. Ferrers two hours, and with my little girle, Mistress Frances Tooker, and very pleasant.

"She isn't so much," he said; but in his heart of hearts he did not believe this.

She is old, but hath, I believe, been a pretty comely woman:

She is our great sweet mother.

She is poor in clothes, and not bred to any carriage, but will be soon taught all, and if Mercer do not come again, I think we may have her upon better terms, and breed her to what we please.

She is pretty, and a girl for that, and her relations, I love.

She is pretty, and a modest, brown girle.

She is quite nicey comfy without her outcast man, madame in rue Git-le-Coeur, canary and two buck lodgers.

She is quite weary of the country, but cannot get her husband to let her live here any more, which troubles her mightily.

She is rather lean.

She is reckoned worth L80,000.

She is returning into the North to her children, where, I perceive, her husband hath clearly got the mastery of her, and she is likely to spend her days there, which for her sake I am a little sorry for, though for his it is but fit she should live where he hath a mind.

She is right, our sister.

She is right, our sister.

She is said to be the heroine of some of the adventures.

She is the bride of darkness, a daughter of night.

She is to come next week.

She is very big, and resolves I must be godfather.

She is very ugly, so that I cannot care for her, but otherwise she seems very good.

She is very well got thither, of which I am heartily glad.

She is worth, and will be at her mother's death (who keeps but a little from her), L2500 per annum.

She is wretched poor; and but ordinary favoured; and we fain to lay out seven or eight pounds worth of clothes upon her back, which, methinks, do go against my heart; and I do not think I can ever esteem her as I could have done another that had come fine and handsome; and which is more, her voice, for want of use, is so furred, that it do not at present please me; but her manner of singing is such, that I shall, I think, take great pleasure in it.

She is yours!

She joined the Church of Rome in 1669, and died March 31st, 1671.

She jumped up and called them and she ran down the slope past him, tossing her hair behind her which had a good enough colour if there had been more of it but with all the thingamerry she was always rubbing into it she couldn't get it to grow long because it wasn't natural so she could just go and throw her hat at it.

"She just feels a little curious, I guess," ventured Minnie.

She just put on more airs about it.

(SHE KEENS WITH BANSHEE WOE)

She kept a servant and developed rapidly in household tactics and information.

She kept him at a distance in a rather earnest way, and submitted only to those tender tokens of affection which better become the inexperienced lover.

She kept him at such lengths as she could, because her thoughts were with her own triumph.

She kicked the bucket.

She killed my hand all right.

She kissed me.

She kissed me.

"She kissed the boy, and said, caressing him, 'It is for thine own dear sake. Thou wilt be faithful, little Charles?'"

She kisses his lips; he kisses hers; they solemnly bless each other.

She knew at once.

She knew from the first poor little Rudy wouldn't live.

She knew full well that Miss Pross was the family's devoted friend; Miss Pross knew full well that Madame Defarge was the family's malevolent enemy.

She knew he meant the monkey was sick.

She knew I, I think she knew by the way she.

She knew it could not last much longer.

She knew nothing of Henderson nor of the methods of applying, but she instinctively felt that this would be a likely place, and accordingly strolled about in that neighbourhood.

She knew nothing of you.

She knew now that she did not like him.

She knew right well, no-one better, what made squinty Edy say that because of him cooling in his attentions when it was simply a lovers' quarrel.

She knew she had to do something.

She knew she was going too far, but her feminine love of finery prevailed.

She knew that he had stormed out.

She knew that out in Chicago this very day the same factory chamber was full of poor homely-clad girls working in long lines at clattering machines; that at noon they would eat a miserable lunch in a half-hour; that Saturday they would gather, as they had when she was one of them, and accept the small pay for work a hundred times harder than she was now doing.

She knew that she had improved in appearance.

She knew that she was to pay four dollars for her board and room, and now she felt that it would be an exceedingly gloomy round, living with these people.

She knew there was no need of calling there now.

She knew what it was to meet with people who were indifferent, to walk alone amid so many who cared absolutely nothing about you.

She laid down her knitting, and began to pin her rose in her head-dress, before she looked at the figure.

She laid her head upon her father's breast, as she had laid his poor head on her own breast, long, long ago.

She lapped slower, then licking the saucer clean.

She laughed: --O wept! Aren't men frightful idiots? With sadness.

She layeth her hands to the spindle, and her hands hold the distaff.

She lays eggs for us.

She lay still.

SHE LEADS HIM TOWARDS THE STEPS, DRAWING HIM BY THE ODOUR OF HER ARMPITS, THE VICE OF HER PAINTED EYES, THE RUSTLE OF HER SLIP IN WHOSE SINUOUS FOLDS LURKS THE LION REEK OF ALL THE MALE BRUTES THAT HAVE POSSESSED HER.)

She leaned back far to look up where the fireworks were and she caught her knee in her hands so as not to fall back looking up and there was no-one to see only him and her when she revealed all her graceful beautifully shaped legs like that, supply soft and delicately rounded, and she seemed to hear the panting of his heart, his hoarse breathing, because she knew too about the passion of men like that, hotblooded, because Bertha Supple told her once in dead secret and made her swear she'd never about the gentleman lodger that was staying with them out of the Congested Districts Board that had pictures cut out of papers of those skirtdancers and highkickers and she said he used to do something not very nice that you could imagine sometimes in the bed.

She leaned on the sideboard watching.

She learned what the theatrical papers were, which ones published items about actresses and the like.

She left L800 a year jointure, a son to inherit the whole estate.

She left to enter Sir William Penn's service.

She let herself be asked for expenses.

She lies in good state, and very pretty she is, but methinks do every day grow more and more great, and a little too much, unless they get more money than I fear they do.

She lies laid out in stark stiffness in that secondbest bed, the mobled queen, even though you prove that a bed in those days was as rare as a motorcar is now and that its carvings were the wonder of seven parishes.

She lies sunk, with her round-house above water.

She liked mignonette.

She liked nice clothes and urged for them constantly.

She liked this little gaslight soldier.

(SHE LIMPS OVER TO THE TABLE.

She lingered for a week.

She lingered in the jewelry department.

She listened until her misgivings vanished.

She listens.

She listens with big dark soft eyes.

She little knew the trivial authority of this individual, or that had there been a vacancy an actor would have been sent on from New York to fill it.

She lived as much in these things as in the realities which made up her daily life.

She lives in Leeson park with a grief and kickshaws, a lady of letters.

She'll be back shortly.

She'll be good, sir.

Shells.

(SHELLS INCLUDED)

She'll look better there than the woman you've got.

She loathed that sort of person, the fallen women off the accommodation walk beside the Dodder that went with the soldiers and coarse men with no respect for a girl's honour, degrading the sex and being taken up to the police station.

She longed and longed and longed.

She longed to be renowned like others, and read with avidity all the complimentary or critical comments made concerning others high in her profession.

She longed to go.

She looked.

She looked about and picked a jacket like the one which she had admired at The Fair.

She looked about and tried to assure herself with the sight of a dozen such details, but, alas, the secondary thought arrived.

She looked and saw before her a man who was most gracious and sympathetic, who leaned toward her with a feeling that was a delight to observe.

She looked an old woman, but was young.

She looked around elsewhere, but it was from the outside.

She looked around her upon the rooms, out of which the evening light was dying, and wondered why she did not feel quite the same towards them.

She looked around to see who it could be.

She looked as if she thought he had been contracting some needless expense.

She looked as though she was dearly loved and her every wish gratified.

She looked at her watch, and it was twenty minutes past two.

She looked at him a moment, meeting his glance, and a light broke in upon her.

She looked at him, and he laughed reassuringly.

She looked at him consciously, expecting something else.

She looked at him the same evening she had made up her mind to go, and now he seemed not so shiftless and worthless, but run down and beaten upon by chance.

She looked at him quizzically, but melted with sympathy as the value of the look upon his face forced itself upon her.

She looked at his hand.

She looked at it while he put up his purse.

She looked at the blue sky overhead with more realisation of its charm than had ever come to her before.

She looked at the little slip bearing her sister's address and wondered.

She looked at the long receding rows of lamps and studied the dark, silent houses.

She looked at these things with certain misgivings.

She looked away, pleased that he should speak thus, longing to be equal to this feeling written upon her countenance.

She looked back at him, mewing.

She looked back up the lighted step, and then affected to stroll up the street.

She looked down, and for the first time felt the pain of not understanding.

She looked fine.

She looked for no refuge in that direction.

- She looked for nothing save what might come legitimately and without the appearance of special favour.

- She looked helplessly around, and then, seeing herself observed, retreated.

- She looked in her purse to leave it.

- She looked in the mirror and pursed up her lips, accompanying it with a little toss of the head, as she had seen the railroad treasurer's daughter do.

- She looked into her glass and saw a prettier Carrie than she had seen before; she looked into her mind, a mirror prepared of her own and the world's opinions, and saw a worse.

- She looked mighty out of humour, and had a yellow plume in her hat (which all took notice of), and yet is very handsome, but very melancholy: nor did any body speak to her, or she so much as smile or speak to any body.

- She looked more practically upon her state and began to see glimmerings of a way out.

- She looked much at what she could see of the Hudson from her west windows and of the great city building up rapidly on either hand.

- She looked quite smart.

- She looked refreshed--more delightful than ever, but reserved.

- She looked simple and charming enough to strengthen the daring of any lover.

She looked so beautiful in the purity of her faith in this lost man, that her husband could have looked at her as she was for hours.

She looked the picture of despair.

She looked the well-groomed woman of twenty-one, and Mrs. Vance praised her, which brought colour to her plump cheeks and a noticeable brightness into her large eyes.

She looked toward the manager's box for a moment, caught his eye, and smiled.

She looked within and without herself in a half-dazed way.

She looketh well to the ways of her household, and eateth not the bread of idleness.

She looks well, sang well, and very merry we were for half an hour.

She loosened many a man's thighs.

She lost her colour, and the old and intent expression was a constant, not an occasional, thing; otherwise, she remained very pretty and comely.

She loved him tenderly, and thinking that it was the last time she should ever speak to him, she told him 'That the concern he showed for her death was enough to make her quit life with regret; but that not possessing charms sufficient to merit his tenderness, she had at least the consolation in dying to give place to a consort who might be more worthy, of it and to whom heaven, perhaps, might grant a blessing that had been refused to her.'

She loved him the more for thinking that he would rescue her so.

She loved to modulate her voice after the conventional manner of the distressed heroine, and repeat such pathetic fragments as appealed most to her sympathies.

She loved to read poetry and when she got a keepsake from Bertha Supple of that lovely confession album with the coralpink cover to write her thoughts in she laid it in the drawer of her toilettable which, though it did not err on the side of luxury, was scrupulously neat and clean.

She loves to be taken dressing herself, as I always find her.

She loves to be taken dressing herself, as I always find her.

She loves to be taken dressing herself, as I always find her.

She loves to be taken dressing herself, as I always find her; and there, after a little talk, to please her, about her husband's pension, which I do not think he will ever get again, I away thence home, and all the afternoon mighty busy at the office, and late, preparing a letter to the Commissioners of Accounts, our first letter to them, and so home to supper, where Betty Turner was (whose brother Frank did set out toward the East Indies this day, his father and mother gone down with him to Gravesend), and there was her little brother Moses, whom I examined, and he is a pretty good scholar for a child, and so after supper to talk and laugh, and to bed.

Shelter, for the night.

She made a very average looking shop-girl with the exception of her features.

She made her way homeward, thinking about her absence.

She made it charming enough, but could not make it delight her.

She made no answer.

She made no answer, because she could think of nothing to say.

She made no answer, but he felt his victory.

She made no answer, but looked steadily toward the window.

She made no answer to this.

She made one more vain effort and then burst into tears.

She made the average feminine distinction between clothes, putting worth, goodness, and distinction in a dress suit, and leaving all the unlovely qualities and those beneath notice in overalls and jumper.

She makes mighty moan of the badness of the times, and her family as to money.

She maketh fine linen, and selleth it; and delivereth girdles unto the merchant.

She maketh herself coverings of tapestry; her clothing is silk and purple.

Shem, Arphaxad, Shelah, Eber, Peleg, Reu, Serug, Nahor, Terah, Abram; the same is Abraham.

She married, 1. Robert Rich, grandson and heir to Robert, Earl of Warwick, on November 11th, 1657, who died in the following February; 2. Sir John Russell, Bart.

She married, secondly, George Rodney Bridges, son of Sir Thomas Bridges of Keynsham, Somerset, Groom of the Bedchamber to Charles IL, and died April 20th, 1702.

She may ask for Mr. Jarvis Lorry, or she may only ask for a gentleman from Tellson's Bank.

She may change her mind.

She may not eat of any thing that cometh of the vine, neither let her drink wine or strong drink, nor eat any unclean thing: all that I commanded her let her observe.

She meant to go home and practise her evolutions as prescribed.

She met a few young men who belonged to Lola's staff.

She met girls at the high school whose parents were truly rich and whose fathers had standing locally as partners or owners of solid businesses.

She met girls of her own age, who looked at her as if with contempt for her diffidence.

She met with painful rebuffs, the most trying of which had been in a manufacturing cloak house, where she had gone to the fourth floor to inquire.

She might be here weeks without getting another one.

She might be here with a ribbon round her neck and do the other thing all the same on the sly.

She might be put in even if she did not have any experience.

She might have been said to be imagining herself in love, when she was not.

She might find another and better later.

She might like something tasty.

She mightn't like me to come that way without letting her know.

"She might think a thousand things," Carton said, "and any of them would only add to her trouble."

She might think it was contrived, in case of the worse, to convey to him the means of anticipating the sentence.

She mighty pressing for a new pair of cuffs, which I am against the laying out of money upon yet, which makes her angry.

She moved her arm.

She moved her hand towards his lips, but he took it in his, and repeated the word.

She moved through the thick throng of strangers, utterly subdued in spirit.

She moved to and fro, in deep and varied thoughts, while the minutes slipped away and night fell completely.

She [Mrs. Ferrers] lies in, in great state, Mr. G. Montagu, Collonel Williams, Cromwell that was, [Colonel Williams-

-"Cromwell that was"--appears to have been Henry Cromwell, grandson of Sir Oliver Cromwell, and first cousin, once removed, to the Protector. He was seated at Bodsey House, in the parish of Ramsey, which had been his father's residence, and held the commission of a colonel. He served in several Parliaments for Huntingdonshire, voting, in 1660, for the restoration of the monarchy; and as he knew the name of Cromwell would not be grateful to the Court, he disused it, and assumed that of Williams, which had belonged to his ancestors; and he is so styled in a list of knights of the proposed Order of the Royal Oak. He died at Huntingdon, 3rd August, 1673. (Abridged from Noble's "Memoirs of the Cromwells," vol. i., p. 70.)--B.] and Mrs. Wright as proxy for my Lady Jemimah, were witnesses.

She [Mrs. Turner] says that he was a pityfull [fellow] when she first knew them; that his lady was one of the sourest, dirty women, that ever she saw; that they took two chambers, one over another, for themselves and child, in Tower Hill; that for many years together they eat more meals at her house than at their own; did call brothers and sisters the husbands and wives; that her husband was godfather to one, and she godmother to another (this Margaret) of their children, by the same token that she was fain to write with her own hand a letter to Captain Twiddy, to stand for a godfather for her; that she brought my Lady, who then was a dirty slattern, with her stockings hanging about her heels, so that afterwards the people of the whole Hill did say that Mrs. Turner had made Mrs. Pen a gentlewoman, first to the knowledge of my Lady Vane, Sir Henry's lady, and him to the knowledge of most of the great people that then he sought to, and that in short his rise hath been his giving of large bribes, wherein, and she agrees with my opinion and knowledge before therein, he is very profuse.

(SHE MURMURS)

She must.

She must and should be his.

She must have been thinking of someone else all the time.

She must look for work.

She needed a hat first of all.

She needed both advantages, for the marks of gripping fingers were deep in her face, and her hair was torn, and her dress (hastily composed with unsteady hands) was clutched and dragged a hundred ways.

She needed clothes.

"She needn't have gone away," he said.

She needn't see me.

"She needn't see me," he answered, sullenly.

She never abated the piercing quality of her shrieks, never stumbled in the distinctness or the order of her words.

She never let them in, he cried again through his laughter as he stamped on gaitered feet over the gravel of the path.

"She never missed before," says a knitting-woman of the sisterhood.

She never wearied of wondering where the people in the cars were going or what their enjoyments were.

She nobly answered: with a gentleman friend.

She nodded, reddening and closing tight her lips.

She noticed, also, that he did not suggest many amusements, said nothing about the food, seemed concerned about his business.

She noticed, also, that his interest in her was a far-off one.

She noticed his pleasant and contented manner, his airy grace and smiling humour, and it merely aggravated her the more.

She noticed suddenly that Mrs. Vance's manner had rather stiffened under the gaze of handsome men and elegantly dressed ladies, whose glances were not modified by any rules of propriety.

She noticed that men and women were smiling.

She noticed that they were pleased, and thoughts of her sister's home and the meal that would be awaiting her quickened her steps.

She noticed these things almost unconsciously.

She now felt that life was better, that it was livelier, sprightlier.

She now read it, and it was so piquant, and wrote in English, and most of it true, of the retiredness of her life, and how unpleasant it was; that being wrote in English, and so in danger of being met with and read by others, I was vexed at it, and desired her and then commanded her to tear it.

She now turned and looked upon him in full, the instincts of self-protection and coquetry mingling confusedly in her brain.

She obeyed not the voice; she received not correction; she trusted not in the LORD; she drew not near to her God.

She often looked at them dreamily when she went there for a certain purpose and felt her own arms that were white and soft just like hers with the sleeves back and thought about those times because she had found out in Walker's pronouncing dictionary that belonged to grandpapa Giltrap about the halcyon days what they meant.

She often said she'd like to visit.

She only basked in the warmth of his feeling, which was as a grateful blaze to one who is cold.

She only felt that she must be careful, and that Hurstwood had an indefinable fascination for her.

She only found the whole situation bitter, and hated him for it thoroughly.

She only knew of the position which Mr. Hale occupied, but, of all things, she did not wish to encounter that personage, on account of her intimacy with his wife.

She only knew that there had been an attack upon the prisons, that all political prisoners had been in danger, and that some had been dragged out by the crowd and murdered.

She only looked an order.

She only looked vaguely into the street.

She only took his affection to be a fine thing, and appended better, more generous results accordingly.

She only turned her head toward the window, where outside all was black.

She, on the contrary, was not at all inclined to accept anything less than a complete fulfilment of the letter of their relationship, though the spirit might be wanting.

She opened her purse and laid down a half dollar.

She openeth her mouth with wisdom; and in her tongue is the law of kindness.

"She ought not to be in comedy," he said.

"She oughtn't to be thinking about spending her money on theatres already, do you think?" he said.

She ought to.

"She ought to keep it for a time, anyhow," said Hanson.

She owed something to Drouet, she thought.

She owes it to me.

"She owes me something to eat," he said.

She paid half of the six dollars with her friend.

She passed a remark.

She passed, not answering.

She passed out with her basket and a marketnet: and Father
 Conmee saw the conductor help her and net and basket
 down: and Father Conmee thought that, as she had nearly
 passed the end of the penny fare, she was one of those good
 souls who had always to be told twice BLESS YOU, MY
 CHILD, that they have been absolved, PRAY FOR ME.

(SHE PATS HIM)

(SHE PATS HIM OFFHANDEDLY WITH VELVET PAWS)

She paused and wrung her little hands.

She paused at the sound of the last two words and wrung her
 hands.

She paused only a moment, and then moved toward the door.

(SHE PAWS HIS SLEEVE, SLOBBERING)

(SHE PEERS AT HIS HANDS ABRUPTLY)

She perceiveth that her merchandise is good: her candle goeth
 not out by night.

She, perhaps, was piqued at Lord Hinchingbroke's refusal
 "to compass the thing without consent of friends" (see
 February 25th), whence her expression, "indifferent" to
 have her.

Shepherd his pipe.

She picked that knowledge up fast enough for herself.

"She picks up her part quick enough."

She pictured herself already appearing in some fine performance on Broadway; of going every evening to her dressing-room and making up.

(SHE PLOPS SPLASHING OUT OF THE WATER)

Sheply being gone, there come the flageolet master, who having had a bad bargain of teaching my wife by the year, she not practising so much as she should do, I did think that the man did deserve some more consideration, and so will give him an opportunity of 20s. a month more, and he shall teach me, and this afternoon I begun, and I think it will be a few shillings well spent.

She pointed an almost accusing hand toward her lover.

(SHE POINTS.

(SHE POINTS TO HIS FOREHEAD)

She, poor wretch, [A new light is thrown upon this favourite expression of Pepys's when speaking of his wife by the following quotation from a Midland wordbook: "Wretch, n., often used as an expression of endearment or sympathy. Old Woman to Young Master: 'An"ow is the missis to-day, door wretch?' Of a boy going to school a considerable distance off 'I met 'im with a bit o' bread in 'is bag, door wretch'" ("A Glossary of Words and Phrases used in S.E. Worcestershire," by Jesse Salisbury. Published by the English Dialect Society, 1894).] was surprized with it, and made me no answer all the way home; but there we parted, and I to the office late, and then home, and without supper to bed, vexed.

She possessed an innate taste for imitation and no small ability.

She poured again a measureful and a tilly.

She poured in a teacup tea, then back in the teapot tea.

She poured more tea into her cup, watching it flow sideways.

She practised her part ruefully, feeling that she was effectually shelved.

She praised the goodness of the milk, pouring it out.

(SHE PRAYS)

She presented her part with some felicity, though nothing like the intensity which had aroused the feeling at the end of the long first act.

She presented herself to me as the wife of the Marquis St. Evremonde.

She presents the curious anomaly of the most solid masonry joining with oak and hemp in constituting the completed ship.

She pretty?

She promised that my boy, every morning, should be carried to the hill to catch the first glimpse of his father's sail!

She proposed to earn her living honestly.

She proposed to make the best of the situation until Drouet left again.

She proves a very fine lady, and mother to fine children.

She provided: at quarter day or thereabouts if or when
   purchases had been made by him not for her she showed
   herself attentive to his necessities, anticipating his desires.

SHE PUFFS CALMLY AT HER CIGARETTE.)

She put an arm round the little mariner and coaxed winningly:
   --What's your name? Butter and cream?

She put her hand to the nail, and her right hand to the
   workmen's hammer; and with the hammer she smote
   Sisera, she smote off his head, when she had pierced and
   stricken through his temples.

She put her needless candle in the shadow at a distance, crept
   up to his bed, and put her lips to his; then, leaned over him,
   and looked at him.

She put her two hands together in her customary expressive way
   and pressed her fingers.

She put her two little hands together and pressed them
   appealingly.

She put it back, and proceeded to get dinner early and in good
   time.

She put most of her spare money in clothes, which, after all, was
   not an astonishing amount.

She put on her hat and fidgeted around the table in the little
   bedroom, wondering where to slip the note.

She put on her hat so that she could see from underneath the
   brim and swung her buckled shoe faster for her breath
   caught as she caught the expression in his eyes.

She put on nine pounds after weaning.

She put out her foot and looked at her shoe reflectively.

(SHE PUTS OUT HER HAND INQUISITIVELY)

(SHE PUTS THE POTATO GREEDILY INTO A POCKET THEN LINKS HIS ARM, CUDDLING HIM WITH SUPPLE WARMTH.

She put the comether on him, sweet and twentysix.

She put the first nail in his coffin.

She quailed as she thought of the insignificance of the amount and rejoiced because the rent was paid until the end of the month.

She quickly brought them down and handed them in;--and immediately afterwards leaned against the door-post, knitting, and saw nothing.

She quite forgot him until about to come out, after the show, when the chance of his being there frightened her.

She quite forgot Hurstwood's presence at times, and looked away to homely farmhouses and cosey cottages in villages with wondering eyes.

She radiated much of the pleasure which her undertakings gave her.

She raised a gloved hand to her hair.

She raised her small gloved fist, yawned ever so gently, tiptapping her small gloved fist on her opening mouth and smiled tinily, sweetly.

(SHE RAISES HER BLACKENED WITHERED RIGHT ARM SLOWLY TOWARDS STEPHEN'S BREAST WITH OUTSTRETCHED FINGER)

She ran with long gandery strides it was a wonder she didn't rip up her skirt at the side that was too tight on her because there was a lot of the tomboy about Cissy Caffrey and she was a forward piece whenever she thought she had a good opportunity to show and just because she was a good runner she ran like that so that he could see all the end of her petticoat running and her skinny shanks up as far as possible.

She reached in her purse and took out one of the bills.

She read "Dora Thorne," or had a great deal in the past.

She read from the manner of Hanson, in the subdued air of Minnie, and, indeed, the whole atmosphere of the flat, a settled opposition to anything save a conservative round of toil.

She read or had read to her his chapbooks preferring them to the MERRY WIVES and, loosing her nightly waters on the jordan, she thought over HOOKS AND EYES FOR BELIEVERS' BREECHES and THE MOST SPIRITUAL SNUFFBOX TO MAKE THE MOST DEVOUT SOULS SNEEZE.

She ready; and, taking some bottles of wine, and beer, and some cold fowle with us into the coach, we took coach and four horses, which I had provided last night, and so away.

She realised that she was a novice, and felt as if a rebuff were certain.

She realized that hers was not to be a round of pleasure, and yet there was something promising in all the material prospect he set forth.

She realized that she was of interest to him from the one standpoint, which a women both delights in and fears.

She really did not care whether he came home any more or not.

She really did not see anything clearer than before, but she was getting into that frame of mind where, out of sympathy, a woman yields.

She really was not enamoured of Drouet.

She rebuked me for doing it, saying that did I do so much to many bodies else it would be a stain to me.

She recalled, with more subtle emotions, that he did not look at her now with any of the old light of satisfaction or approval in his eye.

She received the answer in silence and backed awkwardly out.

(SHE RECLINES HER HEAD, SIGHING)

SHE REGARDS IT AND BLOOM WITH DUMB MOIST LIPS.)

She relaxed a little and let the situation endure, giving him strength.

She relegated her hoop and skippingrope to a recess.

She remembered a few things Drouet had done, and now that it came to walking away from him without a word, she felt as if she were doing wrong.

She remembered having received her first one far back in Columbia City.

She remembered his fine appearance the days he had met her in the park.

She remembered Mrs. Vance, who had never called again after Hurstwood's reception, and Ames.

She remembered now a hundred things that indicated as much.

She remembered: on the 27th anniversary of his birth she presented to him a breakfast moustachecup of imitation Crown Derby porcelain ware.

She remembered that she was hungry and went to the little cupboard in the rear room where were the remains of one of their breakfasts.

She repeated in the same tone, sunk to a whisper, "I have been free, I have been happy, yet his Ghost has never haunted me!"

She reproached me but I had rather talk with any body than her, by which I find I think she is jealous of my freedom with Ashwell, which I must avoid giving occasion of.

She resolved to find out more.

She resolved to spend her money for clothes quickly, before something terrible happened.

She restrained herself with difficulty from showing a quaver in her voice.

She resumed her knitting and went out.

She retired to her chateau at Colombes, near Paris, where she died in August, 1669, after a long illness; the immediate cause of her death being an opiate ordered by her physicians.

She returned and stood in the door.

She reverted to the things which were best and saddest within the small limit of her experience.

Sheriffs did endeavour to get one jewell.

Sheriffs did endeavour to get one jewell.

Sheriffs did endeavour to get one jewell.

She riseth also while it is yet night, and giveth meat to her household, and a portion to her maidens.

She rolled downhill at Rialto bridge to tempt me with her flow of animal spirits.

She rolled up her knitting when she had said those words, and presently took the rose out of the handkerchief that was wound about her head.

She rose.

She rose and closed her reading, rose of Castile: fretted, forlorn, dreamily rose.

She rose and we to dinner, after dinner up to my chamber, where she entertained me with what she hath lately bought of clothes for herself, and Damask linnen, and other things for the house.

She rubbed her handglass briskly on her woollen vest against her full wagging bub.

(SHE RUBS SIDES WITH HIM)

She rummaged her brain for a reason.

(SHE RUNS TO STEPHEN.

(SHE RUNS TO THE PIANOLA)

(SHE RUSHES OUT)

She's a.

She's a bit imbecillic.

She's a friend of one of our members.

She's a gamey mare and no mistake.

She said good-bye with feigned indifference.

She said, 'He is gone; but I cannot tell whither.'

She said, however, that the cognac was flattered, and took up her knitting.

She said, in a low, distinct, awe-stricken voice, as if she were saying it in a dream, "I am going to see his Ghost! It will be his Ghost--not him!"

She said it aloud, but added to herself, as she resumed her knitting: "Hah! Good day, age about forty, height about five feet nine, black hair, generally rather handsome visage, complexion dark, eyes dark, thin, long and sallow face, aquiline nose but not straight, having a peculiar inclination towards the left cheek which imparts a sinister expression! Good day, one and all!"

"She said it was high time."

She said it would look nice over the bed.

She said moreover unto him, We have both straw and provender enough, and room to lodge in.

She said, No man, Lord.

She said nothing more then, objecting to giving up her own money, and yet feeling that such would have to be the case.

She said she thought she'd call here some day.

"She said she was going down to the foot of the stairs," answered Minnie.

She said that he had a fair sweet death through God His goodness with masspriest to be shriven, holy housel and sick men's oil to his limbs.

She said that her father had spoken of hiring a lodging for a short term, in that Quarter, near the Banking-house.

She said thereto that she had seen many births of women but never was none so hard as was that woman's birth.

She sails to-day.

She saith unto him, Grant that these my two sons may sit, the one on thy right hand, and the other on the left, in thy kingdom.

She saith unto him, Yea, Lord: I believe that thou art the Christ, the Son of God, which should come into the world.

She saith unto them, Because they have taken away my LORD, and I know not where they have laid him.

She sat down in one of the rocking-chairs, while Hurstwood waited for the boy, who soon knocked.

She sat meditating, merely shaking her head.

She sat with Minnie, in the kitchen, holding the baby until it began to cry.

She saw a large, empty, shadowy play-house, still redolent of the perfumes and blazonry of the night, and notable for its rich, oriental appearance.

She saw a tight, hard, wiry woman before her, as Mr. Lorry had seen in the same figure a woman with a strong hand, in the years gone by.

She saw design in deeds and phrases which sprung only from a faded appreciation of her presence.

She saw herself in a score of pathetic situations in which she assumed a tremulous voice and suffering manner.

She saw him into and out of the world.

She saw it through a mist of fancy--a pale, sombre half-light, which was the essence of poetic feeling.

She saw no place which did not hold a couple or a group of girls, and being too timid to think of intruding herself, she sought out her machine and, seated upon her stool, opened her lunch on her lap.

She saw one stop and the footman dismount, opening the door for a gentleman who seemed to be leisurely returning from some afternoon pleasure.

She saw only their workday side.

She saw that he himself was hesitating, and with a woman's intuition realised that there was no occasion for great alarm.

She saw that she was taken to be of the same sort and addressed accordingly.

She saw that she would first need to get work and establish herself on a paying basis before she could think of having company of any sort.

She saw that they were privileged and deferred to.

She saw the earrings, the bracelets, the pins, the chains.

She saw "The Royal Charles" brought into the river by them; and how they shot off their great guns for joy, when they got her out of Chatham River.

She saw the servant working at dinner with an indifferent eye.

She saw what Drouet liked; in a vague way she saw where he was weak.

She saw where she had put herself in a peculiar light, namely, that of agreeing to marry when she was already supposedly married.

She says she did give him a very warm answer, such as he did not excuse himself by saying that he said this in jest, but told her that since he saw what her mind was he would say no more to her of it, and desired her to make no words of it.

She says she doubts my father is in want of money, for rents come in mighty slowly.

She says she's making twelve, but that wouldn't buy all those things.

She says that their son, Mr. William Pen, did tell her that his father did observe the commanders did make their addresses to me and applications, but they should know that his father should be the chief of the office, and that she hath observed that Sir W. Pen never had a kindness to her son, since W. Pen told her son that he had applied himself to me.

She's beastly dead.

She's been long getting round to it, hasn't she?

She's better where she is, he said kindly.

She scaled just eleven stone nine.

She scarcely gave a thought to the complication which would trouble her when he was gone.

"She's clever, though," said Drouet, casting off any imputation against Carrie's ability.

She scribbled three figures on an envelope.

She's drunk.

She sealed and addressed the letter, and going in the front room, the alcove of which contained her bed, drew the one small rocking-chair up to the open window, and sat looking out upon the night and streets in silent wonder.

"She's easier," thought Hurstwood to himself.

She seeketh wool, and flax, and worketh willingly with her hands.

She seemed a creature afar off--like every other celebrity he had known.

She seemed a thorough master of her mood—thoroughly confident and determined to wrest all control from him.

She seemed so experienced and self- reliant in her tinsel helmet and military accoutrements.

She seemed the most passionate mourner in the world.

She seemed the one ray of sunshine in all his trouble.

She seemed to be gaining feeling, now that the play was drawing to a close and the opportunity for great action was passing.

She seemed to be talking in her sleep.

She seemed to have so many dainty little things which Carrie had not.

She seemed to have some power back of her actions.

She seemed to me a very comely woman: but I hope to see more of her on Mayday.

She seemed too simple, too yielding.

She seemed to raise it (the listener's eyes were always on his paper), and to let it fall with a rattle on the ledge before her, as if the axe had dropped.

She seemed to realise it in a sort of pussy-like way and instinctively concluded to cling with her soft little claws to Carrie.

She seemed to recede, and now it was difficult to call to her.

She seems a very debonaire, but plain lady.

She seems, by her discourse, to be grave beyond her bigness and age, and exceeding well bred as to her deportment, having been a scholar in a school at Bow these seven or eight years.

She seems sad.

She sees but one object of supreme compliment in this world, and that is herself.

(SHE SEIZES BLOOM'S COATTAIL)

(SHE SEIZES FLORRY AND WALTZES HER.)

She's engaged for a big tour end of this month.

She sent out her boughs unto the sea, and her branches unto the river.

She serves me at his beck.

She set free sudden in rebound her nipped elastic garter smackwarm against her smackable a woman's warmhosed thigh.

She set the brasses jingling as she raised herself briskly, an elbow on the pillow.

Shes faithfultheman.

"She's frightened," whispered Drouet to Hurstwood.

She's game.

She's getting a start now.

"She's going along with me this time," said Drouet.

She's going to sing at a swagger affair in the Ulster Hall, Belfast, on the twenty-fifth.

She's good looking.

She's got to do all right.

She shall be brought unto the king in raiment of needlework: the virgins her companions that follow her shall be brought unto thee.

She shall give to thine head an ornament of grace: a crown of glory shall she deliver to thee.

She, she, she.

She shewed me a letter to my father from my uncle inviting him to come to Brampton while he is in the country.

She's his wife.

She shook her head.

She shook her head.

She shook her head.

She shook her head.

She shook her head as if in deep thought.

She shook her head in absolute misery.

She shook her head negatively.

She shook her head, though for all her distress and his trickery she was beginning to notice what she had always felt—his thoughtfulness.

She shook it off and ate.

She shouted in his ear the tidings.

(SHE SHOUTS)

(SHE SIDLES FROM HER NEWLAID EGG AND WADDLES OFF)

She sighed as she thought of her handsome adorer.

She sighed "No."

She sighs.

She sincerely wished he could get through the summer.

(SHE SINGS)

(SHE SIGNS WITH A WAGGLING FOREFINGER)

She's in the lying-in hospital in Holles street.

She sipped distastefully her brew, hot tea, a sip, sipped, sweet tea.

She sits.

She sits.

She's lame!

She slipped a hand into her kerchief pocket and took out the wadding and waved in reply of course without letting him and then slipped it back.

She's making for Bullock harbour.

"She's making more than she says," thought Hurstwood.

She smelt an onion.

She smiled at Carrie good-naturedly as she passed, showing pretty, even teeth, and Carrie smiled back.

She smiled into his eyes.

She smiled on him.

She smiled to think that men should suddenly find her so much more attractive.

She smilesmirked supercilious (wept! aren't men?), but, lightward gliding, mild she smiled on Boylan.

She's my own true wife I haven't seen for seven years now, sailing about.

SHE SNAKES HER NECK, NESTLING. STEPHEN GLANCES BEHIND AT THE SQUATTED FIGURE WITH ITS CAP BACK TO THE FRONT.)

(SHE SNEERS)

She's not exactly witty.

She's not here.

She's not here.

She's not nicelooking, is she?

"She's not so inexperienced as she looks," he thought, and thereafter his respect and ardour were increased.

She's not well.

She so cruel a hypocrite that she can cry when she pleases.

She so cruel a hypocrite that she can cry when she pleases.

She so cruel a hypocrite that she can cry when she pleases.

She sold lovephiltres, whitewax, orangeflower.

She's on the job herself tonight with the vet her tipster that gives her all the winners and pays for her son in Oxford.

She soon withdrew them, however, and retreated a few feet to rest against the window-sill.

She's passed.

She's passing now.

She's right after all.

She's singing, yes.

"She's some cheap professional," she gave herself the satisfaction of thinking, and scorned and hated her accordingly.

She staid a little at my house, and then walked through the garden, and took water, and went first on board the King's pleasure boat, which pleased her much.

She's taking it all in.

She standeth in the top of high places, by the way in the places of the paths.

She stands.

She started out, weak as ever, but suddenly her nerve partially returned.

She started slightly at the announcement, but told the girl to say that she would come down in a moment, and proceeded to hasten her dressing.

She started to go, and then bethought herself.

She's three days bad now.

She still looked about her upon the great maze of the city without understanding.

She still took a faint pride in him, which was augmented by her desire to have her social integrity maintained.

She stirred in aggravation as she said this.

She stirred uneasily.

She stood immovable close to the grim old officer, and remained immovable close to him; remained immovable close to him through the streets, as Defarge and the rest bore him along; remained immovable close to him when he was got near his destination, and began to be struck at from behind; remained immovable close to him when the long-gathering rain of stabs and blows fell heavy; was so close to him when he dropped dead under it, that, suddenly animated, she put her foot upon his neck, and with her cruel knife--long ready--hewed off his head.

She stood, like a spirit, beside him, and he bent over his work.

She stood outside the shop in sunlight and sauntered lazily to the right.

She stood still, waiting, while the man, husband, brother, like her, searched his pockets for change.

She stood up from her stool and worked that way for a while, but it was a more difficult position.

She stood, very much frightened, awaiting some one.

"She's too gay," said Hurstwood, significantly.

"She's too nervous," said Drouet, feeling in the mildness of the remark that he was lying for once.

She stopped in the act of putting the note in her bosom, and, with her hands yet at her neck, looked terrified at Madame Defarge.

She strained her eyes, but could not make sure.

(SHE STRETCHES UP TO LIGHT THE CIGARETTE OVER THE FLAME, TWIRLING IT SLOWLY, SHOWING THE BROWN TUFTS OF HER ARMPITS.

She stretcheth out her hand to the poor; yea, she reacheth forth her hands to the needy.

She subsequently kept the Rein Deer Inn at Bishops Stortford, at which the Vice-Chancellor, and some of the heads of colleges, had occasion to sleep, in their way to London, and were nobly entertained, their supper being served off plate.

She subsequently married Beau Fielding, whom she prosecuted for bigamy.

She suited action to word, fastened the piece of leather, which was eventually to form the right half of the upper of a man's shoe, by little adjustable clamps, and pushed a small steel rod at the side of the machine.

She, supposing him to be the gardener, saith unto him, Sir, if thou have borne him hence, tell me where thou hast laid him, and I will take him away.

She's waiting for me, I know.

She swallowed a draught of tea from her cup held by nothandle and, having wiped her fingertips smartly on the blanket, began to search the text with the hairpin till she reached the word.

She's well nourished, I tell you.

"She's well," returned Carrie, answering the last query.

(SHE SWISHES HER HUNTINGCROP SAVAGELY IN THE AIR)

She swore to him as they mingled the salt streams of their tears that she would ever cherish his memory, that she would never forget her hero boy who went to his death with a song on his lips as if he were but going to a hurling match in Clonturk park.

She's worth ten, fifteen, more, a pound.

(SHE TAKES HIS HAND)

SHE TAUNTS HIM.)

She tells me, and I find true since, that the House this day have voted that the King be desired to demand right for the wrong done us by the Dutch, and that they will stand by him with their lives fortunes: which is a very high vote, and more than I expected.

She tells me as a secret that Betty Howlet of the Hall, my little
   sweetheart, that I used to call my second wife, is married
   to a younger son of Mr. Michell's (his elder brother, who
   should have had her, being dead this plague), at whichI am
   glad, and that they are to live nearer me in Thames Streete,
   by the Old Swan.

She tells me he hath lost L140 per annum, but have seven
   houses left.

She tells me how Smith, of the Duke's house, hath killed a man
   upon a quarrel in play; which makes every body sorry, he
   being a good actor, and, they say, a good man, however this
   happens.

She tells me how the lifeguard, which we thought a little
   while since was sent down into the country about some
   insurrection, was sent to Winchcombe, to spoil the tobacco
   there, which it seems the people there do plant contrary to
   law, and have always done, and still been under force and
   danger of having it spoiled, as it hath been oftentimes, and
   yet they will continue to plant it.

She tells me how there is a sad house among her friends.

She tells me mighty news, that my Lady Castlemayne is mightily
   in love with Hart of their house: and he is much with her
   in private, and she goes to him, and do give him many
   presents; and that the thing is most certain, and Becke
   Marshall only privy to it, and the means of bringing them
   together, which is a very odd thing; and by this means she
   is even with the King's love to Mrs. Davis.

She tells me my aunt is pretty well, yet cannot live long.

She tells me my Lord Rochester is now declaredly out of hopes of Mrs. Mallett, and now she is to receive notice in a day or two how the King stands inclined to the giving leave for my Lord Hinchingbroke to look after her, and that being done to bring it to an end shortly.

She tells me my song, of "Beauty Retire" is mightily cried up, which I am not a little proud of; and do think I have done "It is Decreed" better, but I have not finished it.

She tells me of a Court like to be in a little time, which troubles me, for I would not willingly go out of town.

She tells me Pall's business with Ensum is like to go on, but I must give, and she consents to it, another 100.

She tells me she hears and believes it is because he, being now begun to be called on offices, resolves not to take the new oathe, he having formerly taken the Covenant or Engagement, but I think he do very simply and will endeavour for his wife's sake to advise him therein.

She tells me, that about a month ago she [Lady Castlemaine] quickened at my Lord Gerard's at dinner, and cried out that she was undone; and all the lords and men were fain to quit the room, and women called to help her.

She tells me that the Duchesse of Richmond do not yet come to the Court, nor hath seen the King, nor will not, nor do he own his desire of seeing her; but hath used means to get her to Court, but they do not take.

She tells me the ladies are to go into a new fashion shortly, and that is, to wear short coats, above their ancles; which she and I do not like, but conclude this long trayne to be mighty graceful.

She tells me to get out and look for work.

She tells me what a rogue my boy is, and strange things he has been found guilty of, not fit to name, which vexes [me], but most of all the unquiett life that my mother makes my father and herself lead through her want of reason.

She tells us that Catelin is likely to be soon acted, which I am glad to hear, but it is at the King's House.

She tells us that the Queen's sickness is the spotted fever; that she was as full of the spots as a leopard which is very strange that it should be no more known; but perhaps it is not so.

She tendered a coin, smiling boldly, holding her thick wrist out.

She thanked me.

She that hath borne seven languisheth: she hath given up the ghost; her sun is gone down while it was yet day: she hath been ashamed and confounded: and the residue of them will I deliver to the sword before their enemies, saith the LORD.

She then fell into the possession of his brother, Colonel Robert Sidney.

She then placed herself before the door of the chamber which Lucie had occupied.

She then sat down on the stairs a few moments to breathe and to cry, and then got up and hurried away.

"'She--there,' said the child, pointing to a squalid woman in a doorway opposite, who fled suddenly down the street. 'That is old Judas,' said the girl."

She thereupon said no; she would not go to any but where she might teach children, because of keeping herself in use of what things she had earnt, which she do not here nor will there, but only dressing.

She there while I with Balty went and bought a common riding-cloake for myself, to save my best.

She thinks.

She thinks.

She thinks she can act.

She thought a long time about this.

She thought, at first, with the faintest alarm, of being left without money--not of losing him, though he might be going away permanently.

She thought, but made no sign.

She thought desperately upon the subject.

She thought his hair had a touch of grey.

She thought how she should like to tell him—what stress and emphasis she would lend her assertions, how she should drive over this whole affair until satisfaction should be rendered her.

She thought of Drouet looking.

- She thought of going down and buying a few copies of the paper, but remembered that there was no one she knew well enough to send them to.

- She thought of leaving Hurstwood and thus making him act for himself, but he had developed such peculiar traits she feared he might resist any effort to throw him off.

- She thought she had to make some sort of showing in order to retain his interest.

- She thought she missed other things, but could not be sure.

- She thought she understood.

- She thought you wanted a cheese HOLLANDAIS.

- She tied a knot with flashing eyes, as if it throttled a foe.

- She timidly laid her hand on his dear breast, and put up a prayer that she might ever be as true to him as her love aspired to be, and as his sorrows deserved.

- She to her mother's and I to Westminster Hall, where I found a full term, and here I went to Will's, and there found Shaw and Ashwell and another Bragrave (who knew my mother wash-maid to my Lady Veere), who by cursing and swearing made me weary of his company and so I went away.

- She told me also of a play shortly coming upon the stage, of Sir Charles Sidly's, which, she thinks, will be called "The Wandering Ladys," a comedy that, she thinks, will be most pleasant; and also another play, called "The Duke of Lerma;" besides "Catelin," which she thinks, for want of the clothes which the King promised them, will not be acted for a good while.

She told him.

She told this Lord that all the jewells she ever had given her at Court, or any other presents, more than the King's allowance of L700 per annum out of the Privypurse for her clothes, were, at her first coming the King did give her a necklace of pearl of about L1100 and afterwards, about seven months since, when the King had hopes to have obtained some courtesy of her, the King did give her some jewells, I have forgot what, and I think a pair of pendants.

She told this Lord that she had reflected upon the occasion she had given the world to think her a bad woman, and that she had no way but to marry and leave the Court, rather in this way of discontent than otherwise, tha the world might see that she sought not any thing but her honour; and that she will never come to live at Court more than when she comes to town to come to kiss the Queene her Mistress's hand: and hopes, though she hath little reason to hope, she can please her Lord so as to reclaim him, that they may yet live comfortably in the country on his estate.

She told me as she was going out again that there was nobody there, and that she came for a sheet of paper.

She told me how she could not come to me this afternoon, but promised another time.

She told me many things very discreetly, and said she had all his papers and books, and key of his cutting house, and showed me a bag which I and Wm. Joyce told, coming to L5 14s. 0d., which we left with her again, after giving her good counsel, and the boys, and seeing a nurse there of

Mrs. Holden's choosing, I left them, and so walked home greatly troubled to think of my brother's condition, and the trouble that would arise to me by his death or continuing sick.

She told us that Mr. Montagu is to return to Court, as she hears, which I wonder at, and do hardly believe.

She to Mr. Hunt's, and I to White Hall Chappell, and then up to walk up and down the house, which now I am well known there, I shall forbear to do, because I would not be thought a lazy body by Mr. Coventry and others by being seen, as I have lately been, to walk up and down doing nothing.

She too.

She, too, could act appealingly.

She took a folded postcard from her handbag.

SHE TOOK A PENKNIFE OUT OF HER POCKET
AND CUT OFF HIS LITTLE HEAD.

She took back the card, sighing.

SHE TOOK HIM BY THE LILYWHITE HAND
AND LED HIM ALONG THE HALL
UNTIL SHE LED HIM TO A ROOM
WHERE NONE COULD HEAR HIM CALL.

She took his first embraces.

She took it for granted that the doctor had really seen her husband, and that he had been riding, most likely, with some other woman, after announcing himself as BUSY to her.

She took it to heart as a creditable thing, until he added: "That puts a burden of duty on you. It so happens that you have this thing. It is no credit to you--that is, I mean, you might not have had it. You paid nothing to get it. But now that you have it, you must do something with it."

She took no notice while he read by rote a solfa fable for her, plappering flatly: --Ah fox met ah stork. Said thee fox too thee stork: Will you put your bill down inn my troath and pull upp ah bone?

She took occasion to talk of her sister Wight's making much of the Wights, who for namesake only my uncle do shew great kindness to, so I fear may do us that are nearer to him a great deal of wrong, if he should die without children, which I am sorry for.

She took only a mouthful to eat and then practised on, sustained by visions of freedom from financial distress-- "The sound of glory ringing in her ears."

She took physique also to-day, and both of our physiques wrought well, so we passed our time to-day, our physique having done working, with some pleasure talking, but I was not well, for I could make no water yet, but a drop or two with great pain, nor break any wind.

She took the car and arrived at Ogden Place in three-quarters of an hour, but decided to ride on to the West Side branch of the Post-office, where she was accustomed to receive Hurstwood's letters.

She took the letter the next morning, and at the corner dropped it reluctantly into the letter-box, still uncertain as to whether she should do so or not.

(SHE TOSSES A PIECE.

(SHE TRACES LINES ON HIS HAND)

She tried to answer, but he turned away and shuffled off toward the east.

She tried to be calm and indifferent, but it was a palpable sham.

She tried to console herself with the thought that a score of other persons, men and women, were equally tremulous concerning the outcome of their efforts, but she could not disassociate the general danger from her own individual liability.

She tried to think she could to it.

She tripped along, the clear sky pouring liquid blue into her soul.

She troubled herself no more upon the matter.

She troubled herself over what else to put in the letter.

She trudges, schlepps, trains, drags, trascines her load.

She truly pitied this sad, lonely figure.

She trusts me, her hand gentle, the longlashed eyes.

She turned about and fixed on Carrie a very searching eye.

She turned about, troubled by her daring, glad of her release, wondering whether she would get something to do, wondering what Drouet would do.

She turned and recognised him on the instant.

She turned back, resolving to hunt up Storm and King and enter.

She turned her head as the carriage came up to her, rose quickly, and presented herself at the carriage-door.

She turned herself, and saith unto him, Rabboni; which is to say, Master.

She turned out a cruel deceiver.

She turned over sleepily that time.

She turned slowly toward the audience without seeing.

She turned to slip on her jacket.

She turned upon him, animal-like, able to strike an effectual second blow.

SHE TURNS AND, HOLDING OUT HER HANDS, DRAWS HIM OVER.

(SHE TURNS UP BLOOM'S HAND)

She twentythree.

She twisted and turned from one position to another slightly different, but it did not ease her for long.

She understands all she wants to.

She understood little of political complications, internal, or balance of power, external.

She understood well enough what it meant.

She undid her broad lace collar before the mirror and unfastened her pretty alligator belt which she had recently bought.

She unloosed her hair after a time, and let it hang in loose brown waves.

She used her feet less heavily, a thing that was brought about by her attempting to imitate the treasurer's daughter's graceful carriage.

She used the word devil, which vexed me.

She used the word devil, which vexed me.

She used the word devil, which vexed me.

She used to be a tasty dresser.

"She used to be quite a beauty."

She used to look over some nights when Molly was in the Coffee Palace.

She used to say Ben Dollard had a base barreltone voice.

(SHE WAILS)

She waited until the whole department was aware of her presence.

She walked bravely forward, led by an honest desire to find employment and delayed at every step by the interest of the unfolding scene, and a sense of helplessness amid so much evidence of power and force which she did not understand.

She walked by this institution several times hesitating, but, finding herself unobserved, faltered past the screen door and stood humble waiting.

She walked deliberately through the door and up to the gentleman, who looked at her weary face with partially awakened interest.

She walked east along Van Buren Street through a region of lessening importance, until it deteriorated into a mass of shanties and coal-yards, and finally verged upon the river.

She walked in imitation of her mentor as requested, inwardly feeling that there was something strangely lacking.

She walked into the wholesale district, but as the thought of applying came with each passing concern, her heart shrank.

She walked on and on, and finally did go into one place, with the old result.

She walked out into the busy street and discovered a new atmosphere.

She walked with a certain quiet dignity characteristic of her but with care and very slowly because--because Gerty MacDowell was ...

She wandered about after the dishes were put away, talked a little with Minnie, and then decided to go down and stand in the door at the foot of the stairs.

She wandered about, assuring herself that she was making up her mind to look for something, and at the same time feeling that perhaps it was not necessary to be in such haste about it.

She wandered through the whole scene between herself and the intruding villain, straining the patience of the audience, and finally exiting, much to their relief.

She wanted him to know just how well she was doing.

She wanted pleasure, she wanted position, and yet she was confused as to what these things might be.

She wanted something, but no man should buy her by false protestations or favour.

She wanted to be good-natured and sympathetic, but something about the man held her aloof.

She wanted to get out quickly, because she knew but few, and the stars were gossiping.

She wanted to know what this peculiar action of his imported.

She wanted to make some reference to their relations upon the train, but was too timid.

She wanted to take her sufferings, whatever they were, in such a world, or failing that, at least to simulate them under such charming conditions upon the stage.

She wanted to think.

She was …

She was about to retort but something checked the words on her tongue.

She was absolutely without pity.

She was a cold, self-centred woman, with many a thought of her own which never found expression, not even by so much as the glint of an eye.

She was a daughter of …

She was affable, vain, subject to flattery, and this combination, he knew quite well, might produce a tragedy in a woman of her home position.

She was again the victim of the city's hypnotic influence.

She was a gay little Manon, unwitting of society's fierce conception of morality, but, nevertheless, good to her neighbour and charitable.

She was a golden-haired doll!

She was a good, compassionate lady, and not happy in her marriage.

She was a good girl.

She was alive with feeling, her eyes snapping, her lips quivering, her whole body sensible of the injury she felt, and partaking of her wrath.

She was all at sea mentally, and fearful of some entanglement which might ensue from what she would answer.

She was, all in all, exceedingly happy.

She was alone; she was desireful; she was fearful of the whistling wind.

She was alone, very much alone.

She was also to look after a necklace of pearle, which she is mighty busy about, I being contented to lay out L80 in one for her.

She was always a swell-looker, and he had tried to put on the air of being worthy of such as she, in front of her.

She was a mischievous newsmonger, and was keenly wondering what the effect of her words would be.

She was--and He was--before the slow years of the North Tower--ages ago.

She was angry, mortified, grief-stricken.

She was a nice old bag of tricks.

She was apparelled like any barbaric Ethiopian emperor, his neck heavy with pendants of polished ivory.

She was a ship of the old school, rather small if anything; with an old-fashioned claw-footed look about her.

She was asked the same old questions with which she was already familiar.

She was a sweet little mortal to him--there was no doubt of that.

She was as yet more drawn than she drew.

She was a thing of trophies.

She was attached to the court of the Princess of Orange, daughter of Charles I., 1654, and contracted to James, Duke of York, at Breda, November 24th, 1659.

She was a womanly woman not like other flighty girls unfeminine he had known, those cyclists showing off what they hadn't got and she just yearned to know all, to forgive all if she could make him fall in love with her, make him forget the memory of the past.

She was a woman upon whose action under provocation you could never count.

She was a work-seeker, an outcast without employment, one whom the average employee could tell at a glance was poor and in need of a situation.

She was barr'd up in whale-bones, that did leese
None of the whale's length, for they reached her knees;
Off with her head, and then she hath a middle
As her waste stands, just like the new found fiddle,
The favourite Theorbo, truth to tell ye,
Whose neck and throat are deeper than the belly.

She was beginning to see now that he knew something.

She was beginning to weary.

She was being pleaded with, persuaded, led into denying old rights and assuming new ones, and yet there were no words to prove it.

She was betrothed to a good young man, too: a tenant of his.

She was bound up completely in the man's atmosphere.

She was brought to bed in St. Sepulchre's parish of two children; one is dead, the other is alive; her name Elizabeth, and goes by the name of Taylor, daughter to John Taylor.

She was buried, September 12th, in the church of St. Denis.

She was busy adjusting her thoughts and feelings to newer conditions, and was not in danger of suffering disturbing pangs from either quarter.

She was capital.

She was carrying things with too high a hand.

She was certain there was more behind it all than what she had heard, and evil curiosity mingled well with distrust and the remnants of her wrath of the morning.

She was completely restored and delighted by his consideration, but she made him promise not to come around.

She was concentrating herself too thoroughly--what she did really required less mental and physical strain.

She was constantly pained by the sight of the white-faced, ragged men who slopped desperately by her in a sort of wretched mental stupor.

She was created with that passivity of soul which is always the mirror of the active world.

She was crying in her wretched bed.

She was daughter of the Duke de Medina Sidonia and widow of Juan IV.

She was deeply rejoicing in her affection for Hurstwood and his love, and looked forward with fine fancy to their next meeting Sunday night.

She was delicately moulded in sentiment, and answered with vague ruminations to certain wistful chords.

She was depending for her enjoyment upon the Vances.

She was determined, and had worsted him in a very important contest.

She was determined now, however, that her husband was a brute, and that, under no circumstances, would she let this go by unsettled.

She was determined now to have a try at the fascinating game.

She was distracted and uncertain, deciding and doing things without an aim or conclusion, and she had not the slightest conception of how the whole difficulty would end.

She was dressing herself by the fire in her chamber, and there took occasion to show me her leg, which indeed is the finest I ever saw, and she not a little proud of it.

She was drifting mentally, unable to say to herself what to do.

She was eighteen years or age, bright, timid, and full of the illusions of ignorance and youth.

She was elated and began figuring at once.

She was engaged in looking out of the window.

She was entitled to her widow's dower At common law.

She was especially gratified to find that her salary was now eighteen instead of twelve.

She was exceedingly wrathful and struck at Hurstwood, who dodged.

She was extremely happy now that she understood.

She was fading, while he was still preening himself in his elegance and youth.

She was far from perfect in household methods and economy, and her little deviations on this score first caught his eye.

She was flushing scarlet to the roots of her hair, but Drouet did not catch the full hue of her face, owing to the modified light of the room.

She was for the moment wholly at sea, anxious to think for herself, and wondering what new deception was this which caused him to give out that she was ill when she was not.

She was frowning.

She was frowning alone on the stage and the audience was giggling and laughing.

She was gazing now sadly out upon the open sea, her arm resting listlessly upon the polished door-post.

She was getting in the metropolitan whirl of pleasure.

She was glad that something told her to put on the transparent stockings thinking Reggy Wylie might be out but that was far away.

She was glad to be out of the flat, because already she felt that it was a narrow, humdrum place, and that interest and joy lay elsewhere.

She was glad when the short half hour was over and the wheels began to whirr again.

"She was good-looking, wasn't she?" said the manager's companion, who had not caught all the details of the game he had played.

She was grateful for the drummer's presence, though.

She was greatly distressed.

She was humming.

She was in a front row, by the side of a man whom he had never seen since his arrival at the Barrier, but whom he directly remembered as Defarge.

She was in a most helpless plight.

She was in a night-robe and dressing-gown, with her hair very much tousled, but she looked so pretty and good-natured that Carrie instantly conceived a liking for her.

- She was in a position to become refractory with considerable advantage, and Hurstwood conducted himself circumspectly because he felt that he could not be sure of anything once she became dissatisfied.

- She was in a soft clinging white in a studied attitude and the gentleman was in chocolate and he looked a thorough aristocrat.

- She was in a tremble of excitement and opposition as she spoke.

- She was in great agitation.

- She was in her new suit of black sarcenet and yellow petticoat very pretty.

- She was in no mood, after her failure of the day before, to hasten forth upon her work-seeking errand, and yet she rebuked herself for what she considered her weakness the day before.

- She was interesting, in a manner, to the occupant of the chair, and the simplicity of her request and attitude took his fancy.

- She was interred in January, 1457, in the Chapel of Our Lady, at the east end of this church; but when that building was pulled down by her grandson, Henry VII., her coffin was found to be decayed, and her body was taken up, and placed in a chest, near her first husband's tomb.

- She was in the high school, and had notions of life which were decidedly those of a patrician.

She was keenly aware of all the little things that were done—the little genuflections and attentions of the waiters and head waiter which Americans pay for.

She was known as "La belle Henriette."

She was leading the field.

She was left standing, gazing nervously upon the floor.

She was left to herself to brood and wonder.

She was letting her few supports float away from her.

She was listening, smiling, approving, and yet not finally agreeing.

She was looking for something which would calm her conscience, and here it was, a light, airy disregard of her claims upon his justice.

She was making a most miserable showing, and yet feelings were generating within her which were anything but crumbling cowardice.

She was manned almost wholly by Polynesians.

She was merely a servant to him now, nothing more.

She was mightily pleased to have your message, when I gave it her.

She was mighty angry with me, that in all this time I never writ to her, which I do think and take to myself as a fault, and which I have promised to mend.

She was more clever than he.

She was more hopeless than Mrs. Morgan, who had recovered somewhat, and was now saying her lines clearly at least.

She was more inexpressibly sad than she had ever been in life.

She was more than the old Carrie to Drouet.

She was nearly beside herself, and almost hugged Lola, who clung to her at the news.

She was no longer ordered, but requested, and that politely.

She was no more: the trembling skeleton of a twig burnt in the fire, an odour of rosewood and wetted ashes.

She was nonplussed at the possibility of the errand being different from what she had thought.

She was no sensualist, longing to drowse sleepily in the lap of luxury.

She was no talker.

She was not aware of his presence until he was quite near her.

She was not contrasting it now with what she had had, but what she had so recently seen.

She was not exactly sure what she thought of him--what she wanted to do.

She was not going to be a common shop-girl, she thought; they need not think it, either.

She was not going to be dragged into poverty and something worse to suit him.

She was nothing--absolutely nothing at all.

She was not hungry at all, but weak, and her eyes were tired, straining at the one point where the eye-punch came down.

She was not in his life, nor any of the things that touched his life, and yet now, as he spoke of these things, they appealed to her.

She was not in the way.

She was not like the common run of store-girls.

She was not ready to begin to-day, but do to-morrow.

She was not silly, and yet attention of this sort had its weight.

She was not so dull but that she could perceive they were but three small rooms in a moderately well-furnished boarding-house.

She was not supposed to be inconsolable, and scandal followed her at the court of Charles II., where she died of small-pox, December 24th, 1660.

She was not sure, after it was all over, just how the trouble had begun.

She was not sure but that he might call anyhow Monday night, and, while she felt a little disturbed at the possibility, there was, nevertheless, just the shade of a wish that he would.

She was not the kind to be seriously disturbed by his actions.

She was not unfrequently the victim of this disorder, and she called it, in familiar conversation, "a fit of the jerks."

She was not used to slang.

She was not used to this type, and felt that there was something hard and low about it all.

She was not very strong, and sitting all day affected her back.

She was not without realisation already that this thing was impossible, so far as she was concerned.

She was now a thin, though rugged, women of twenty-seven, with ideas of life colored by her husband's and fast hardening into narrower conceptions of pleasure and duty than had ever been hers in a thoroughly circumscribed youth.

She was now experiencing the first shades of feeling of that subtle change which removes one out of the ranks of the suppliants into the lines of the dispensers of charity.

She was now one of a group of oriental beauties who, in the second act of the comic opera, were paraded by the vizier before the new potentate as the treasures of his harem.

She wasn't in a hurry either.

She wasn't silly.

She was one of those who worked at the machines in the shoe factory.

She was opening her purse, and now pulled out all the bills in it--a five and two twos.

She was pale and trembling.

She was perfectly certain that here was happiness.

She was perfectly willing that he should enjoy himself in his way, but she did not care to be neglected herself.

She was pleased in part that the streets were bright and clean.

She was pleased to see her in a way but reflected her husband's point of view in the matter of work.

She was pretty enough to have been married long ago.

She was pretty, graceful, rich in the timidity born of uncertainty, and with a something childlike in her large eyes which captured the fancy of this starched and conventional poser among men.

She was pretty, yes, indeed!

She was pushing at his knees, but he only pulled her back.

She was pronounced beautiful by all who knew her though, as folks often said, she was more a Giltrap than a MacDowell.

She was quite alone.

She was quite appalled at the man's audacity.

She was quite disturbed for the moment as to her appearance, but soon satisfied herself by the aid of the mirror, and went below.

She was Rachel, weeping for her children, because they were not.

She was rather dazed by the assault.

She was reading the card, propped on her elbow.

She was realising now what it was to be petted.

She was relieved to see that he felt nothing.

She was ripened by it in spirit for many suggestions.

She was rocking, and beginning to see.

She was sad beyond measure, and yet uncertain, wishing, fancying.

She was saved in that she was hopeful.

She was secretly somewhat pleased by the fact that much of her husband's property was in her name, a precaution which Hurstwood had taken when his home interests were somewhat more alluring than at present.

She was shrewd.

She was sitting, rocking and thinking, and did not care to have her enticing imaginations broken in upon; so she said little or nothing.

She was slightly flurried and tingling in the cheeks, but it was more nervousness than either fear or favour.

She was slightly taken back at the overtures of a well-dressed man of thirty, who in passing looked at her, reduced his pace, turned back, and said: "Out for a little stroll, are you, this evening?"

She was so excited that she got up and tried to get by him again.

She was so ill as to be shaved and pidgeons put to her feet.

She was so ill as to be shaved and pidgeons put to her feet.

She was so ill as to be shaved and pidgeons put to her feet.

She was something to struggle for, and that was everything.

She was somewhere to the northward of the Line.

She was soon lost in the world it represented, and wished that she might never return.

She was so overcome she could not speak.

She was sorry for him, too, with that peculiar sorrow which finds something complimentary to itself in the misery of another.

She was stiff, a little dizzy, and very thirsty.

She was still nervous to reach Drouet and see what could be the matter.

She was still the victim of his keen eyes, his suave manners, his fine clothes.

She was stirred by this thought, angered by that--her own injustice, Hurstwood's, Drouet's, their respective qualities of kindness and favour, the threat of the world outside, in which she had failed once before, the impossibility of this state inside, where the chambers were no longer justly hers, the effect of the argument upon her nerves, all combined to make her a mass of jangling fibres--an anchorless, storm-beaten little craft which could do absolutely nothing but drift.

She was struck as by a blade with the miserable provision which was outside the pale of marriage.

She was struck with the evidences of wealth, although there was, perhaps, not a person on the street worth more than a hundred thousand dollars.

She was sure she had not seen it all--that the city was one whirl of pleasure and delight.

She was surprised at the briefness of the entire part, not knowing that she must be on the stage while others were talking, and not only be there, but also keep herself in harmony with the dramatic movement of the scenes.

She was taken bad on the Tuesday ...

She was the golden thread that united him to a Past beyond his misery, and to a Present beyond his misery: and the sound of her voice, the light of her face, the touch of her hand, had a strong beneficial influence with him almost always.

She was there, sitting beside her father.

She was thinking if she had only herself to support this would leave her seventeen for herself.

She was thinking it was slightly strange.

She was thinking of returning to the flat.

She was thinking this over when she came down to the table, but for some reason the atmosphere was wrong.

She was thrown into a transport by the tidings Mr. Lorry gave her of her husband, and clasped the hand that delivered his note--little thinking what it had been doing near him in the night, and might, but for a chance, have done to him.

She was tired and nervous.

She was to meet him at half-past eight.

She was too busy scrubbing the kitchen woodwork and calculating the purchasing power of eighty cents for Sunday's dinner.

She was too calculating to jeopardize any advantage she might gain in the way of information by fruitless clamour.

She was too full of wonder and desire to be greedy.

She was too much occupied then with fears for the brother who so little deserved her affection, and with Sydney's friendly reassurances, adequately to heed what she observed.

She was too wrought up to care to go down to eat, too pensive to do aught but rock and sing.

She was troubled, and her heart did rise as soon as she appeared, and seems the most ugly woman that ever she saw.

She was truest to them in the season of trial, as all the quietly loyal and good will always be.

She was used to Drouet's appearance.

She was vaguely feeling that she would come in contact with the great owners, that her work would be where grave, stylishly dressed men occasionally look on.

She was very hungry, and the things she saw there awakened her desires, but the high prices held her attention.

She was very much aware that a climax was pending.

She was visited by a young author, who had a play which he thought she could produce.

She was wearing her black and it had the perfume of the time before.

She was wearing the blue for luck, hoping against hope, her own colour and lucky too for a bride to have a bit of blue somewhere on her because the green she wore that day week brought grief because his father brought him in to study for the intermediate exhibition and because she thought perhaps he might be out because when she was dressing that morning she nearly slipped up the old pair on her inside out and that was for luck and lovers' meeting if you put those things on inside out or if they got untied that he was thinking about you so long as it wasn't of a Friday.

She was well primed with a good load of Delahunt's port under her bellyband.

She was wondering what Drouet had told him, what her attitude would be.

She was wondering what she could do.

She was wondering whether he took her to be a millionaire.

She was wondering why that miserable thought must be brought in.

She was worth it.

She waved about her outspread INDEPENDENT, searching, the lord lieutenant, her pinnacles of hair slowmoving, lord lieuten.

She waved her scarf and cried: Huzzah! Sceptre wins!

She waved, unhearing Cowley, her veil, to one departing, dear one, to wind, love, speeding sail, return.

She wavered, totally unable to make a move.

Shewed him Mr. Coventry's sense of it, which he sent me last post much to my satisfaction.

Shewed, like a wise man, that righteousness is a surer moral way of being rich, than sin and villainy.

She weepeth sore in the night, and her tears are on her cheeks: among all her lovers she hath none to comfort her: all her friends have dealt treacherously with her, they are become her enemies.

She went about among the glass cases and racks where these things were displayed, and satisfied herself that the one she thought of was the proper one.

She went again, and in so doing temporarily recovered her equanimity.

She went away, and I staid a good while after, and was seen going out by one of our neighbours near the office and two of the Hall people that I had no mind to have been seen by, but there was no hurt in it nor can be alledged from it.

She went foolishly out, the office boy deferentially swinging the door for her, and gladly sank into the obscuring crowd.

She went home, and I to my lodgings.

She went home rejoicing, knowing that soon something must come of it.

She went hunting aimlessly through the crowded columns.

She went on thinking this, answering vaguely, languishing affectionately, and altogether drifting, until she was on a borderless sea of speculation.

She went over the tangle again and again.

She went over the whole ground in Hurstwood's absence, and discovered little objections that had not occurred to her in the warmth of the manager's argument.

She went over to the dresser and struck a match, lighting the gas.

She went slowly down the stairs.

She went thither, I to Mr. Crew's, where I dined and my Lord at my Lord Montagu of Boughton in Little Queen Street.

She went to bed one night before Hanson.

She went to one of the great department stores and bought herself one, using a dollar and a quarter of her small store to pay for it.

She went upstairs, where everything was silent.

She went with Mr. Child to Whitehall chapel and Mr. Pierce with me to the Abbey, where I expected to hear Mr. Baxter or Mr. Rowe preach their farewell sermon, and in Mr. Symons's pew I sat and heard Mr. Rowe.

SHE WHIPS IT OFF.)

SHE WHIRLS IT BACK IN RIGHT CIRCLE.

SHE WHIRLS THE PRIZE IN LEFT CIRCLE.

She who made the bed, being privy to his escape, that night, to blind the warder when he came to lock the chamber-door, went to bed, and possessed Colonel Lambert's place, and put on his night-cap.

She will be full of sympathy with its enemies.

She will be home directly, and it is better she should not see us together to-night.

She will be in a state of mind to impeach the justice of the Republic.

She will be mourning and grieving.

She will do him good and not evil all the days of her life.

She will do very well.

She will drown me with her, eyes and hair.

She will have in me a man already pretty well off, and a rapidly rising man, and a man of some distinction: it is a piece of good fortune for her, but she is worthy of good fortune.

She will now be at home, awaiting the moment of his death.

She will put her hands together and pray you to be merciful.

She wished she knew a way out.

Shew me a penny.

Shew me a token for good; that they which hate me may see it, and be ashamed: because thou, LORD, hast holpen me, and comforted me.

Shew me the tribute money.

Shew me thy ways, O LORD; teach me thy paths.

She wondered at her own solitude these two years past--her indifference to the fact that she had never achieved what she had expected.

She wondered at the magnitude of this life and at the importance of knowing much in order to do anything in it at all.

She wondered how he could think to carry himself so in her presence after the cynicism, indifference, and neglect he had heretofore manifested and would continue to manifest so long as she would endure it.

She wondered if she would be with it.

She wondered that he came so frequently, that Mrs. Drouet should go out with him this afternoon when Mr. Drouet was absent.

She wondered what could induce him to go alone.

She won in a thunderstorm, Rothschild's filly, with wadding in her ears.

She won't refuse me a few dollars.

She wore a coquettish little love of a hat of wideleaved nigger straw contrast trimmed with an underbrim of eggblue chenille and at the side a butterfly bow of silk to tone.

She worked about the room until Drouet put in appearance at five o'clock.

She worked, after dressing, to arrange a little breakfast for herself, and then advised with Minnie as to which way to look.

She would be scolded, abused, ignominiously discharged.

She would care for him with creature comforts too for Gerty was womanly wise and knew that a mere man liked that feeling of hominess.

She would fain have cried to him chokingly, held out her snowy slender arms to him to come, to feel his lips laid on her white brow, the cry of a young girl's love, a little strangled cry, wrung from her, that cry that has rung through the ages.

She would fain see me and be at her house again, but we must be content.

She would find out at once just what advantages she could gain.

She would follow, her dream of love, the dictates of her heart that told her he was her all in all, the only man in all the world for her for love was the master guide.

She would get along all right, but where would he be?

She would get in one of the great shops and do well enough until--well, until something happened.

She would get stockings, too, and a skirt, and, and--until already, as in the matter of her prospective salary, she had got beyond, in her desires, twice the purchasing power of her bills.

She would go, and they would be happy.

She would go down in the morning and hunt for work.

She would half confess if she had not all sinned as women did.

She would have a better time than she had ever had before--she would be happy.

She would have adored him.

She would have a far-off thought of Columbia City now and then, or an irritating rush of feeling concerning her experiences of the present day, but, on the whole, the little world about her enlisted her whole attention.

She would have been led into a newer and worse situation.

- She would have been utterly wretched in her fear of not gaining his affection, of losing his interest, of being swept away and left without an anchorage.

- She would have done better if she had not secured a position so quickly, and had seen more of the city which she constantly troubled to know about.

She would have done nearly as well with a block of wood.

She would have given worlds to know what it was.

She would have her work and this.

- She would have known as much if she could have analysed her feelings, but this thing which she now felt aroused by his great feeling broke down the barriers between them.

- She would have me send him to sea; which if I could I would do, but there is no ship going out.

- She would have more lady-like treatment or she would know why.

She would have to come along.

She would have to go home, that was all.

She would have to quit them.

She would have to talk with and explain to him.

She would live in Chicago, her mind kept saying to itself.

She would look at him with large, pleased eyes.

She would look at the jackets.

She would look fine too, if only she had some of these things.

She would make the great sacrifice.

She would marry another.

She would need to save part of the twenty to pay her fare home.

She would not err in any way, if she could help it.

She would not know how, she would not be quick enough.

She would not let him come to bed to her out of jealousy.

She would not let him come to bed to her out of jealousy.

She would not let him come to bed to her out of jealousy.

She would not stay in the fright.

"She wouldn't write at all if she didn't care for me."

She would prevaricate, but it would be in the line of her feelings at least.

She would see Hurstwood no more.

She would speak for that when silent on all else.

She would stand and bite her lips as they passed, shaking her little head and wondering.

She would take the envelope and know that she had triumphed.

She would tell him that it was all over between them.

She would try to understand him because men were so different.

She would wait and brood, studying the details and adding to them until her power might be commensurate with her desire for revenge.

She would write him and let him know what she thought.

She writes.

She writes word how the Joyces grow very rich and very proud, but it is no matter, and that there was a talk that I should be knighted by the King, which they (the Joyces) laugh at; but I think myself happier in my wife and estate than they are in theirs.

Shew the things that are to come hereafter, that we may know that ye are gods: yea, do good, or do evil, that we may be dismayed, and behold it together.

Shew thy marvellous lovingkindness, O thou that savest by thy right hand them which put their trust in thee from those that rise up against them.

Shew us thy mercy, O LORD, and grant us thy salvation.

www.ingramcontent.com/pod-product-compliance
Lightning Source LLC
Chambersburg PA
CBHW051652040426
42446CB00009B/1094